SUPREME® BAR REVIEW

Contracts & Sales

Bar Exam Review

Supreme Bar Review
30539 Pinetree Road, Suite 224
Cleveland, Ohio 44124

(866) BAR-PREP (toll-free)

SupremeBarReview.com

Printed in the United States of America.

ISBN-13: 978-1-936450-02-2

For information address:

Supreme Bar Review
30539 Pinetree Road, Suite 224
Cleveland, Ohio 44124

SupremeBarReview.com

TABLE OF CONTENTS

I. CONTRACTS IN GENERAL

A. GOVERNING LAW

On the bar exam, you will be presented with questions that must be answered under either the common law of contracts, or under the Uniform Commercial Code. Generally, contracts are governed by the common law. However, contracts for the sale of goods (i.e., things other than land, services, or intangible personal property) are governed by Article 1 (General Provisions) and Article 2 (Sales) of the Uniform Commercial Code (UCC), as well as the common law.

B. DEFINITION

A contract is a **promise** or set of promises that **the law will enforce** through a legal or equitable remedy. Contract liability is based on the voluntary assent of the parties.

C. TYPES OF CONTRACTS

1. **Express Contracts.** Contracts may be express, through an explicit or formal expression of voluntary agreement;

2. **Contracts Implied in Fact.** Contracts may be implied in fact, from the conduct of the parties in the context of the circumstances surrounding the conduct; or

3. **Contracts Implied in Law.** Contracts implied in law are not true contracts. A contract implied in law exists when liability is necessary in **restitution** to prevent unjust enrichment even though neither the language nor the conduct of the parties manifests a voluntary agreement.

D. REQUIREMENTS

Contracts require a **legal subject matter**, **mutual assent** via offer and acceptance, and **consideration** or a substitute for consideration such as promissory estoppel. For a contract to be enforceable there must **not** be a valid defense or excuse.

E. CONTRACTS FOR THE SALE OF GOODS GOVERNED BY UCC ARTICLE 2

Article 2 of the Uniform Commercial Code (UCC) applies to any contract for the sale of goods, where ownership of specific goods will be transferred. Goods are things that are moveable at the time for identification of the goods to the contract.

1. **Specially Manufactured Goods.** Contracts for goods to be "specially manufactured" or custom-built, are contracts for the sale of goods, governed by UCC Article 2.

   Example: Window Co. agrees to construct and sell "custom designed and built" windows to Contractor who is in the process of constructing a building for Owner. The contract is one for the sale of goods, governed by UCC Article 2.

2. **Unborn Animals.** Contract for the sale of unborn animals is a contract for the sale of goods under UCC 2-105.

3. **Goods To Be Severed From Realty**: Minerals, structures and crops; other goods removable without material harm to real estate under UCC 2-107.

   a. **Contract for the sale of minerals** (coal, iron ore, oil, gas, etc.), or for a structure (e.g., a shed) is a contract for the sale of goods if the goods are to be severed from the real estate by the seller.

   b. **Contract for the sale of minerals or structure with buyer to remove** the minerals or structure is outside the scope of Article 2 of the UCC and governed by the common law applicable to contracts for the transfer of an interest in real estate.

   c. **Contract for the sale of growing crops** (including timber) is a contract for the sale of goods, regardless of whether buyer or seller will remove the crops from the land.

   d. **Contract for sale of other fixtures or other goods capable of removal** from real estate without material harm to the land is a contract for the sale of goods, regardless of who removes the items.

      Example: A contract for the sale of a built-in oven, which can be removed without causing material harm to the house, is a contract for the sale of goods.

4. **Goods and Services Combined – Hybrid Contracts.** In a "hybrid" contract involving a mix of goods and services, the "predominant purpose" of the contract controls the application of Article 2.

   Note: Even if the dispute focuses on the services feature of the contract, so long as the predominant purpose of the contract is the sale of goods, Article 2 governs.

   a. **Construction Contracts.** UCC Article 2 does not govern construction contracts which include the incorporation of goods.

   b. **Delivery and Installation.** Contracts for the sale of goods, with delivery or minor installation incidental to the sale, are governed by UCC Article 2.

      Example: Contractor agrees to construct a building for Owner. In order to perform, Contractor will necessarily use lumber, concrete, nails, etc., incorporating them in the new building. The contract is one for services, governed by the common law, **not** by UCC Article 2.

      Example: Hardware Store enters into contract with Homeowner for sale, delivery, and installation of a new hot water heater in Homeowner's residence. Although the contract provides for delivery and installation services, the predominant purpose of the contract is for the sale of goods, the hot water heater, and it is thus governed by Article 2 of the UCC.

c. **Food and Drinks.** Contracts for serving of food or drink to be consumed either on the premises, or elsewhere is a sale of goods for purposes of the implied warranty of merchantability under UCC 2-314.

Example: Customer suffers food poisoning from tainted food purchased from and served in a Restaurant. Contract for food is a contract for the sale of goods for purposes of the implied warranty of merchantability. Tainted food is not "fit for the ordinary purpose" and thus there is a breach of the implied warranty of merchantability.

MBE Advice

Once you have determined that a question is based on the law of Contracts, check to see if it is a transaction involving the sale of goods. If so, UCC Article 2 applies.

On the Multistate Bar Exam (MBE), the examiners may try to trick you by offering an incorrect answer choice involving a common law rule that does not apply to the sale of goods. Remember, in contracts for the sale of goods, when Article 2 conflicts with the common law, Article 2 controls.

II. FORMATION OF CONTRACTS

Contracts require mutual assent, usually found through an offer and acceptance, together with consideration or promissory estoppel.

A. MUTUAL ASSENT

In express contracts assent is demonstrated by a **formal offer and acceptance**. In contracts implied in law, assent is demonstrated by **conduct.** Assent can also be found in any conduct that demonstrates the parties' agreement. A precise time of formation of the contract does not need to be determined.

B. OFFER

An offer is an **outward manifestation of assent** that justifies another person in believing that his assent to a bargain is invited and will conclude it. In determining whether there is an offer, the court will examine the language used, the circumstances surrounding the language, and any existing or prior relationship between the parties, including any usage of trade or industry, custom or past performance between the parties.

1. **Power of Acceptance in Offeree**. An offer creates a **power of acceptance** in the person to whom the offer is directed. This power may be exercised by an unequivocal manifestation of assent to the terms of the offer, which is an acceptance.

2. **Communication of Offer Necessary** – To be effective, an offer must be communicated outwardly in a manner which leads the person to whom it is directed to reasonably believe that his assent to a bargain is invited. Subjective intent does not affect formation of a contract.

3. **Preliminary Negotiations**, which do not manifest a willingness to be bound, do not create a contract.

    a. **Advertisements** are not normally considered offers because they are not sufficiently limited in scope. Advertisements of rewards and prizes, however, may be offers where they are adequately limited such as by "first-come, first served". Where an advertisement appears to be sufficiently limited in scope, apply the definition of offer to determine whether the ad may constitute an offer.

    b. **Preliminary Agreements** are not binding where an execution of a formal written contract is understood as a necessary condition to formation of a contract.

        1) **Written Memorial Contemplated**. A contract is formed informally where the parties express their intent to be bound even though they contemplate a subsequent writing to memorialize their agreement. However, where execution of a subsequent memorial is a "condition" upon which the contract depends, there is no contract until the writing is completed.

        2) **Letters of Intent**. "Letters of intent" executed during stages of the negotiation are not binding where they are made expressly conditional on the execution of a later, formal contract after the remaining details have been resolved. However, letters of intent may be binding where the parties have manifested their agreement to be bound and where the remaining details are definite enough that a reasonably certain basis for applying a remedy can be found.

4. **Termination of Offers**: The duration of an offer depends on its terms as expressed by the offeror. The offeror is the "master of the offer" and can specify its duration. The offeree has the power of acceptance and can accept the offer any time prior to its termination. Offers and the offeree's power of acceptance are terminated by Death or Incapacity of the Offeror, Lapse of Time, Rejection, Counteroffer, or Revocation.

    a. **The Death or Incapacity of Offeror**. Death or incapacity of the offeror terminates an offer that has not yet been accepted, despite the offeree's lack of notice.

    b. **Lapse of Time**. An offer terminates after expiration of the time stated in the offer for acceptance. If no time is stated, an offer lapses after a **reasonable time**.

        1) In face-to-face or telephone conversations, an offer lapses at the end of the conversation unless circumstances indicate that the offer remains open beyond the end of the conversation.

2) If the offer specifies a time during which the offer will remain open, that time is a reasonable time; but unless the offer is irrevocable, it may be revoked by the offeror any time before lapse.

c. **Rejection.** Rejection by the offeree terminates the offer.

1) **Rejections Effective Upon Receipt.** A rejection is not effective until it is received by the offeror. When the offeree sends a rejection and subsequently sends an acceptance there is a contract unless the rejection arrives (or the offeror otherwise learns of the rejection) before the acceptance is sent.

Example: Employer sends Worker a letter, offering him employment in a new job for $60,000. Upon receipt, Worker sends a letter declining the offer. A day later, before the Worker's letter declining is received, Worker phones Employer and expresses his acceptance. There is a contract because the acceptance was effective when communicated to the Employer, which was before the letter rejecting the offer was received.

2) **Offer Terminated Upon Rejection.** Once an offer has been rejected, it may not subsequently be accepted unless it is renewed.

Example: Contractor offers to replace Homeowner's roof for $15,000. Homeowner sends a rejection, saying the price is too high, which Contractor receives. A day later, Homeowner changes his mind and sends Contractor a letter agreeing to the $15,000 price. In the meantime, Contractor has taken on other jobs and doesn't want to do the work for any price. There is no contract. Contractor's offer was rejected, ending Homeowner's power of acceptance. Homeowner's letter agreeing to the $15,000 price was a new offer which Contractor can accept, reject, or ignore.

Example: Artist offered to restore Gallery's painting for a price of $5,000. Gallery made a counteroffer, agreeing to pay $4,000 instead. Artist replied: "Price firm, $5,000." Gallery faxed its agreement to pay the $5,000. There is a contract to restore the painting for $5,000. Although Artist's original offer was rejected, because of the Gallery's counteroffer, Artist's reply indicating that the price was firm at $5,000 could have reasonably been understood by Gallery as a renewal of Artist's original offer. Gallery's fax expressed its acceptance of the price.

3) **Inquiry For Details Is Not a Rejection.** A request for clarification of the terms of the offer is not a rejection.

Example: Buyer offers to purchase Owner's house for $100,000, with all fixtures to be included in the sale. Owner asks Buyer if Buyer considers the refrigerator, washer, and dryer to be included as fixtures. The inquiry is not a rejection of the offer and the Owner still has the power to accept.

d. **Counteroffer as Rejection.** A counteroffer by the offeree, on terms different from those contained in the original offer, operates as a rejection of the offer. Thus, "I'll pay $10,000" in response to an offer to sell for $10,500 is a rejection of the original offer.

1) Under the common law **mirror image rule,** an acceptance must be identical to the terms of the offer. If an attempted acceptance includes additional or different terms, it is treated as a **counteroffer** which rejects the terms of the original offer.

2) In a **contract for the sale of goods**, under UCC 2-207, a purported acceptance, which contains terms different from those in the offer, may constitute an acceptance despite different or additional terms, so long as it is a definite and seasonable expression of acceptance or a confirmation sent within a reasonable time of the offer.

3) A **mere inquiry** about other terms, such as "will you consider less?," does not constitute a counteroffer.

e. **Revocation by Offeror.** An offer may be terminated through revocation by the offeror any time prior to its acceptance. Revocation is not effective until received.

1) Revocation is effective when the offeree learns of the offeror's change of intent to enter into the contract.

Example: Homeowner delivers offer to Buyer for sale of Homeowner's house for $150,000, giving Buyer a week to accept. Two days later, Buyer learns from a friend that Homeowner has sold the house to someone else. Buyer attempts to communicate his acceptance to Homeowner. There is no contract between Homeowner and Buyer. Though Homeowner did not communicate the revocation of his offer directly, Buyer nevertheless learned that the offer was no longer open for acceptance, because of the sale to the third person, before Buyer communicated his acceptance.

5. **Irrevocable Offers.** Offers are normally revocable by the offeror anytime prior to acceptance by the offeree. However, offers may become irrevocable under the following circumstances:

a. **Option Contract**. When the offeree has paid for a promise to keep the offer open, there is an option contract. To constitute an option contract there must be consideration for the promise to keep the offer open, usually for a specific time, or if no time is stated, for a reasonable time. When there is consideration for a promise to keep the offer open, it cannot be revoked by the offeror prior to the expiration of the stated time for acceptance. Unless otherwise specified in the offer, acceptance of an option contract is only effective upon receipt.

b. **Firm Offer By Merchant in Sale of Goods Under UCC 2-205.** An offer for the sale of goods, in writing, by a merchant, which contains assurances that it will be kept open, is irrevocable for the time stated, so long as the time is not greater than 3 months. If no time is stated, the offer is irrevocable for a reasonable time, not to exceed 3 months.

Example: In response to inquiry from Builder, Furnace Manufacturer supplies a written bid for the sale of a Heating and Air Conditioning System, indicating that the price of $5,500 will remain open for "2 months from date of bid." One month later, Furnace Manufacturer sends letter indicating "price raised to $6,000." The next day Builder sends letter "accepting" the previously submitted bid for $5,500. There is a contract for sale at $5,500. The offer from Furnace Manufacturer was in writing, Manufacturer is in the business of selling goods of the kind and is thus a merchant, and the offer contained assurances that it would remain open for a specific time period within the 3 month limit set by UCC 2-205. Thus, the offer was not revocable by Manufacturer. Because this is a "firm offer" under UCC 2-205, Builder need not prove that it relied in any way on the assurance that the offer would remain open.

c. **Part Performance by Offeree of Offer for Unilateral Contract**. Part performance of an offer that invites performance as a reasonable method of acceptance makes the offer irrevocable. Mere preparation for performance, however, is not adequate. Thus, efforts to search for the perpetrator of a crime, in an effort to claim a "reward" offered for information leading to the criminal's arrest and conviction, will not make the offer of a reward irrevocable. But partial performance of an offer to "pay $100 if you clean out the gutters on my house" left on a telephone answering machine, will make the offer irrevocable.

d. **Reliance on a Promise That the Offer Will Remain Open.** Where the offeror expressly promises that the offer will remain open for a specific time and the offeree reasonably relies on the promise of irrevocability, the offer is irrevocable.

e. **Foreseeable Reliance.** Where the offeree reasonably and foreseeably relies on an express or implied promise to keep an offer open, the offer is irrevocable. This scenario most frequently arises in "construction" cases involving sub-contracting bids, where sub-contractors submit bids to a general contractor for use by the general in preparing a bid for the entire construction project. There is an implied promise that the sub-contracting bid will remain open for a reasonable time to permit the general to use it in computing his general contracting bid.

Example: Sub-contractor submits bid to a General Contractor with the expectation that the general contractor will rely on the bid in submitting his own general contracting bid. Sub may not revoke the sub-contracting bid where the General has relied on it to his detriment by using it as expected by the sub-contractor. The promise to keep the offer open may be express or implied from the circumstances.

Watch Out!

The first step in the formation of any contract is always for someone to make an offer. Unless you are told in the facts that there is a valid contract, always make sure that the fact pattern contains a valid offer. Without a valid offer there can be no contract.

C. ACCEPTANCE

Acceptance is an unequivocal manifestation of assent to the terms proposed in an offer made by the offeree in the manner authorized by the offer. Acceptance may take the form of a return promise or conduct. Acceptance exercises the "power of acceptance" held by the offeree.

1. **Who May Accept**. Offers may be accepted only by the person to whom the offer was extended. An offer may be accepted by a person who reasonably believes that he or she was the person to whom the offer was extended. This will depend on the manifestation of intent in the offer.

    a. **Advertisements Directed at the General Public** are not normally regarded as offers, but if they are sufficiently limited in scope, as rewards frequently are, they may be accepted by anyone who acts with knowledge of the offer.

    b. **No Assignment of Offer**. An offer or "power of acceptance" may not be assigned.

Watch Out!

There is one *exception* to the general rule that offers may not be assigned: ***option contracts may be assigned.***

2. **Manner of Acceptance**:

    a. An acceptance may be made in **any manner reasonable under the circumstances**. This may include either a return promise or a beginning of performance. However, the offer may expressly limit the manner of acceptance.

        1) Acceptance by mail, "FedEx," fax, phone, telegram, or other reasonably prompt manner is usually sufficient absent circumstances indicating that a more expedient method is required.

        2) **Exclusive Manner of Acceptance Expressed in Offer.** If the offer unequivocally specifies a particular manner of acceptance as the exclusive manner, then acceptance must be made in that manner. However, where possible,

the offer will be construed as suggesting rather than mandating a specific mode of acceptance.

3) **Waiver of Exclusive Manner of Acceptance.** Even where an exclusive method of acceptance is specified, the offeror may expressly or impliedly waive the specified manner.

   Example: Buyer sent offer to Seller, unequivocally specifying that acceptance could be made only by Seller "signing and returning" Buyer's purchase order. Buyer's later acquiescence in Seller's delivery and installation of goods, without the return of signed purchase order, waived the limitation on manner of acceptance expressed in the offer.

b. **Dispatch or "Mailbox" Rule**: When acceptance may be made by a return promise, acceptance is **effective when it is sent**, so long as it is properly addressed or directed.

1) **Improper Address.** An acceptance is not effective upon dispatch if it is not properly addressed to the offeror or, in cases of acceptance via mail, is not accompanied by the necessary postage. If the acceptance is properly delivered, despite the offeree's failure to use the proper address or postage, it will be effective when received.

2) **Effective Only on Receipt in Option Contract.** In an option contract, an acceptance is effective only upon receipt, unless the option contract specifies otherwise.

3) **Offer Specifies Acceptance Effective Only on Receipt.** An offer may specify that acceptance will be effective only upon receipt. If so, the acceptance is not effective on dispatch.

Watch Out!

A typical ***mailbox rule*** fact situation on the bar exam will involve an offeree who cannot seem to make up his or her mind. Watch out for the offeree who sends both an acceptance and a rejection, one after the other:

- If the offeree sends an acceptance followed by a rejection, a valid contract has been formed, unless the offeror receives the rejection first and then acts in detrimental reliance upon the rejection.
- If the offeree sends a rejection followed by an acceptance, there is a valid contract only if the acceptance is received first.

c. **Beginning of Performance as Acceptance.** The beginning of performance, with notice, constitutes acceptance of an offer for a bilateral contract, where beginning performance is a reasonable method of acceptance. **Mere preparations** for beginning performance do not alone constitute acceptance.

1) **Contracts for Sale of Goods.** In contracts for the sale of goods, an offer for prompt or current shipment of goods may be accepted either by a timely promise to ship the goods or by shipment of either conforming or non-conforming goods. UCC 2-206.

d. **Unilateral Contracts – Acceptance Limited to Performance of an Act.** Unilateral contracts are rare. But, where an offer expressly limits the method of acceptance to the performance of an act, completion of the act is the only permissible method of acceptance.

Example: Creditor's offer to take $45,000 in payment of a $48,000 debt if the lower sum is paid by July 10, may not be "accepted" by a promise to pay the smaller sum. The offer may be revoked any time prior to payment. Mere preparation to perform is not sufficient.

1) Notice of performance is usually required. Where performance necessarily conveys notice, no separate notice is necessary, such as where the performance is open and notorious.

2) Notice is not required where the terms of the offer make notice unnecessary.

Example: Offer in an advertisement for "Payment of $100 to anyone who catches the flu after using the Carbolic Smoke-Ball according to instructions" does not require notice of acceptance apart from notice claiming the reward.

3) The beginning of performance, with any necessary notice, is not sufficient to constitute acceptance, but makes the offer irrevocable for a reasonable time for performance to be completed.

Example: Homeowner makes offer to Painter: "I'll pay $4,000 if you paint my house." Painter begins performance by starting to paint. The offer is irrevocable for a reasonable time for Painter to finish the job.

4) Preparations for performance, even with notice, do not constitute part performance.

Example: Homeowner makes an offer to Painter: "I'll pay $4,000 if you paint my house." Painter goes to the paint store and purchases paint, brushes, etc. Homeowner rejects the offer. There is no contract. Though Painter incurred expense in preparing to begin, Painter had not yet started performance. Painter may, however, have a claim, based on reasonable foreseeable reliance, for any unrecoverable value of the paint.

5) True unilateral contracts are unusual. An offer that calls for the beginning of performance is likely to be construed as an offer for a bilateral contract susceptible of acceptance by beginning performance with notice or by a return promise.

Example: Homeowner makes an offer to Painter "I'll pay $4,000 to have my house painted." Painter says: "I'll start tomorrow." There is a contract. Though the offer was phrased in terms indicating that performance was the requested manner of acceptance, the context indicated that Homeowner sought either a return promise or the beginning of performance as a means of acceptance.

e. **Manner of Acceptance of Offers for Sale of Goods under UCC 2-206.** Under UCC 2-206, an offer to buy goods for prompt or current shipment may be accepted by a promise or by the shipment of conforming or non-conforming goods.

1) **The seller's shipment of non-conforming goods:** the shipment is both an acceptance and a breach, unless the seller promptly notifies the buyer that the shipment was made as an "accommodation."

Example: Radio Station orders Transmitter capable of transmitting at 105.3 MHz. Seller responds by shipping Transmitter capable only of transmitting at 103.5 MHz. Seller's shipment of non-conforming goods is an acceptance, and a breach.

Example: Buyer orders red oxford cloth shirt from Seller. Seller promptly ships a "pink" shirt and includes a message indicating that the Seller is out of red shirts and has sent the "pink" shirt as an "accommodation" to the Buyer. The Seller's shipment is a counter-offer which the Buyer may accept or reject. The Seller is not in breach.

f. **Unequivocal Communication.** The offeree's manifestation of acceptance must be unequivocal.

1) **Conditional Acceptance.** An acceptance which imposes conditions or additional or different terms is not an acceptance.

2) A "**grumbling acceptance**" which expresses an unequivocal commitment is effective as an acceptance.

Example: After lengthy negotiations, Contractor offers to construct building for Homeowner for $250,000. Homeowner responds by saying: "I don't really like this very much, but ok, go ahead and start." There is a contract despite Homeowner's expression of reservations. His communication unequivocally expressed his willingness to go ahead with the transaction and thus was an acceptance.

3. **Who May Accept.** Offer may only be accepted by the person to whom it is directed – a person who would reasonably believe that it was directed to him may accept.

4. **Knowledge of Offer Required for Acceptance.** A person must have knowledge of an offer in order to accept. Performance of an act requested in an offer is not acceptance if performed by a person without knowledge of the offer.

   Example: Pet Lover posts signs advertising a $100 reward for the return of his lost cat, Elwood. Neighbor finds and returns a lost animal, without having seen the posted signs and thus without knowledge of an offer of reward. There is no contract; Neighbor did not know of the offer of reward.

   a. "**Crossed offers**" do not create a contract. An exchange of identical offers does not create a contract, despite the appearance of a "meeting of the minds" because an offer cannot be accepted unless the offeree knows it has been made.

      Example: Seller sends letter to Buyer, offering to sell his house for $200,000. At the same time, Buyer sends letter to Seller, offering to buy the property for $200,000. Both parties receive each other's letter. There is no contract. Neither party sent his letter with knowledge of the offer of the other.

5. **Acceptance That Adds Terms: Mirror Image Rule and UCC 2-207.** Under the traditional common law rule an acceptance must be a "mirror image" of the offer. Any additional or different terms will operate as a rejection and a counter-offer. The "last shot" rule results in a contract consisting of the terms last proposed before performance.

   Example: Employer sends letter offering Worker a job for a one-year term at a salary of $50,000, commencing on January 1. Worker sends a letter purporting to "accept," but indicating that he expects to be paid moving expenses in order to relocate. Because the acceptance was not a "mirror image" of the offer, there is not yet a contract. Worker's proposal is a counteroffer which must be accepted by Employer before a contract can be found.

   a. **UCC 2-207 Changes Mirror Image Rule**. In contracts for the sale of goods, the mirror image rule has been abandoned. A "definite and seasonable expression of acceptance" or "written confirmation sent within a reasonable time" is effective as an acceptance even though it contains different or additional terms, so long as it does not make acceptance "expressly conditional on assent to the additional or different terms."

      Example: Buyer sent a purchase order, seeking to buy 1000 widgets for $15 each, for immediate delivery. Upon receipt, Seller sent an acknowledgment, repeating the terms calling for 1000 widgets for $15 each, for immediate delivery, and adding a term excluding liability for any consequential damages. Two days later Seller shipped the goods; upon their arrival Buyer took them and used them for its business. Under common law, the Seller's acknowledgement was a "counteroffer." A contract was not formed until Buyer accepted the goods, upon their arrival. The terms of the contract would have included Seller's exclusion of liability for consequential damages. Under UCC 2-207, Seller's acknowledgement was an acceptance. Under UCC 2-207(2) (discussed below) the term excluding liability for consequential damages is nothing more than a proposal to modify the contract that has not been accepted.

1) **Difference in "Bargained" Terms. UCC 2-207.** There may be no contract if the bargained terms of price, quantity, description and delivery do not match – there is no "definite … expression of acceptance."

2) **Acceptance Expressly Conditional on Assent. UCC 2-207.** In order for a response to be expressly conditional on assent to the new terms, and thus a counter-offer, the offeree must **demonstrate its unwillingness to proceed** with the transaction until the new terms are agreed upon. Part performance, such as by shipping goods ordered by a buyer, demonstrates the seller's willingness to proceed even without agreement to the new terms. Refusal to begin performance is necessary to prevent acceptance.

   Example: Buyer sent purchase order, for 500 gizmos for $10 each, for immediate delivery. Seller's acknowledgment, repeating these terms and adding a term disclaiming the implied warranty of merchantability, further indicated that "acceptance is expressly conditional on assent to the terms contained in this confirmation." Seller then shipped the goods together with a copy of the acknowledgement. After delivery the gizmos exploded resulting in property damage to the Buyer's place of business. A contract exists for sale of the widgets for $10, despite the warranty disclaimer and "acceptance expressly conditional" language in the acknowledgment. The latter language, purporting to make acceptance conditional on assent did not prevent the acknowledgement from operating as an acceptance because Seller, by shipping the goods, failed to demonstrate its unwillingness to proceed with the transaction absent assent to its own terms. Under UCC 2-207(2) (discussed below) the warranty disclaimer is nothing more than a proposal to modify the contract.

b. **Treatment of "Additional or Different Terms."** The additional or different terms do not prevent formation of a contract for the sale of goods under UCC 2-207.

   1) **Additional or Different Terms Proposals for Addition.** Under UCC 2-207, the additional or different terms contained in the acceptance are mere "proposals" for addition to the contract which must be expressly accepted in order to become part of the contract.

2) **Between Merchants the Additional Terms Become Part of the Contract.** Under UCC 2-207 if the transaction is "between merchants" the additional or different terms in the acceptance become part of the contract unless:

   a) the offer expressly limited acceptance to its terms;

   b) the additional terms are a **material alteration** to the contract; or

   c) the offeror objects within a reasonable time to the additional terms.

   Warranty disclaimers, limited remedies, and arbitration clauses are "material alterations."

   Example: Buyer and Seller agreed over the phone for the sale of 1000 cases of electrical components, for a price of $75 per case, for delivery within a week. The next day Seller sent a written confirmation describing the components and repeating agreed upon terms of 1000 cases at $75 per case for delivery within a week. The acknowledgment added language stipulating that any disputes would be resolved by "binding arbitration." Upon timely arrival of the goods Buyer accepted them, but later discovered a latent defect justifying revocation of acceptance. When Seller refused to correct the problem, Buyer sued. Seller sought to dismiss the suit, asserting the provision in its acknowledgment calling for binding arbitration of disputes. The phone conversation resulted in the formation of a contract. Under UCC 2-207(2) the arbitration clause in the Seller's acknowledgment was a proposal for addition to the contract which could become a part of the contract only if the transaction was "between merchants." Even if Buyer and Seller were both merchants, the arbitration clause would not become part of the contract because, as a waiver of a constitutional right to a jury trial, it was a material alteration.

3) **Knock-Out of Different Terms.** Courts have interpreted UCC 2-207 to knock-out different or conflicting terms. When a contract for the sale of goods is formed through an exchange of forms despite the presence of **different terms,** the conflicting terms knock each other out and the contract consists of the terms on which the writings agree, together with the gap-filling terms provided by Article 2 of the UCC. This "knock-out" rule is not expressed in the language of UCC 2-207 but has been developed by courts interpreting its language.

c. **Exchange of Forms Does Not Create Contract.** Under UCC 2-207, where the exchange of forms does not result in a contract, but performance by the parties shows agreement, the contract consists of the terms on which the writings agree plus Article 2's gap filling provisions regarding reasonable price, time for delivery, place of delivery, implied warranties, etc.

6. **Acceptance by Silence.** Silence is not usually effective as acceptance. Silence is acceptance in the unusual circumstance of some prior agreement or course of dealing between the parties that establishes the unequivocal meaning of silence as acceptance.

   a. Agreements with book and CD clubs that the customer's silent failure to return a postcard will constitute acceptance of an offer to sell the book of the month, permits silence to constitute acceptance.

   b. Past conduct between the parties, such as repeated instances of the buyer taking and paying for goods sent by the seller, creating a reasonable expectation that the goods will be paid for absent notice to the contrary, makes silence operate as acceptance.

   c. Under common law, silent acceptance of benefits of performance will also constitute acceptance where a party would be unjustly enriched if contract liability were not imposed. However, U.S. Postal Regulations on "unsolicited merchandise" deprives silent acceptance of goods shipped to a person of its effect.

D. AUCTION SALES OF GOODS UNDER UCC 2-328

1. **Auctions With Reserve.** Auction sales are presumed to be "with reserve." In an auction with reserve, **the auctioneer is permitted to withdraw the goods** anytime prior to an auctioneer's acceptance of a bid via "the fall of the hammer" or in any other customary manner. In such auctions, individual bids are "offers" which the auctioneer may accept or reject.

2. **Auctions "Without Reserve."** In an auction announced or advertised as "without reserve," the "putting up" of the goods for bids is a commitment, irrevocable for a reasonable time, to sell the goods to the highest bidder. The auctioneer may not withdraw the goods after the goods are "put up" and the bidding begins.

3. **Effect of Bids at an Auction for the Sale of Goods.** Under UCC 2-328, a bid is an offer which creates a power of acceptance in the auctioneer on behalf of the seller.

   a. **New Bid Terminates Previous Bid.** Under UCC 2-328 each bid operates to terminate the power of acceptance created by a previous bid. If a bid is made "while the hammer is falling," the auctioneer has the discretion to reopen the bid or declare the goods sold under the bid on which the hammer was falling. If the new bid is recognized, the new bid discharges the previous bid on which the hammer was falling.

   b. **Retraction of Bids.** Under UCC 2-328 auction sale bids may be revoked, prior to the "fall of the hammer" or other customary announcement of the conclusion of the sale, in auctions "with reserve" or "without reserve."

      1) **No Reinstatement of Previous Bids.** Retraction of a bid does not reinstate any previous bid.

E. DEFINITENESS OF TERMS REQUIRED

For a contract to be enforceable, its terms must be definite. It must be sufficiently definite to demonstrate agreement between the parties and to provide a reasonably certain basis for providing a remedy.

1. **Effect of Indefinite Terms on Contract Formation**. The traditional common law rule is that where the subject matter, parties, quantity or other essential terms cannot be reasonably determined, there is no contract. Modern cases and the UCC permit the parties to make a contract with uncertain terms so long as they have expressed an intent to be bound and the terms agreed upon are sufficiently certain to provide a reasonable basis for a remedy. A quantity term is still essential for framing a remedy.

2. **Uncertain Terms Permitted in Contract for Sale of Goods.** UCC 2-204 permits formation of a contract for the sale of goods where the parties have manifested an intent to make a contract and there is a reasonably certain basis for giving an appropriate remedy, even though one or more terms are left open.

   a. **Indefinite Terms Not Fatal To Creation of Contract for Sale of Goods.** The fact that the parties have not agreed on some terms, or have intentionally left some terms to be agreed upon at a later date, does not automatically prevent formation of a contract for the sale of goods under UCC 2-204 so long as there was an intent to be bound and there is a reasonably certain basis for providing an appropriate remedy.

   b. **Intent To Form Contract.** The absence of some terms may indicate a lack of intent to be bound, but UCC 2-204 permits enforcement of a contract, despite gaps in the parties' agreement, so long as they intended to be bound despite the missing terms.

   c. **Reasonably Certain Basis For Providing an Appropriate Remedy**. If the parties have intended to be bound, despite indefinite or undecided terms, the court will find a contract if the agreement is sufficiently definite for the court to apply an appropriate remedy. The UCC provides gap filling terms where the parties have made an agreement despite the absence of certain terms. The gap-filling terms of the UCC can resolve many indefinite terms such as price, time for delivery, and place for delivery. In output and requirements contracts, even the quantity can be supplied.

   d. **Quantity Term**. A quantity term is usually necessary for application of the code's remedy provisions. However, even in the absence of a quantity term, a remedy based on the aggrieved party's expenses incurred in reliance on the contract may be used, so long as the absence of a quantity term did not reflect a lack of intent to be bound.

3. **Gap Filling Terms in UCC Article 2 for Contracts for Sale of Goods.**

   a. **Quantity Term in Requirement and Output Contracts**. Though quantity term must be definite for contract for sale of goods, requirement and output contracts are enforceable under UCC 2-306. In such contracts, the quantity will be determined, with reasonable elasticity, based on **estimates** made by the parties, or, in the absence of stated estimates, **past requirements or output**. The actual quantity may not be unreasonably disproportionate to any stated estimates or prior quantities. The quantity sought in a requirements contract or delivered in an output contract must be the **good faith requirements of the buyer or the good faith output of the seller.**

Example: Seller agreed to deliver to buyer all of its output of "bread crumbs," a manufactured item. The contract is enforceable, based on the seller's good faith output of bread crumbs with the quantity to be determined based on past output. Increased cost of producing the items, even if it means performing the contract at a loss, will not justify the seller in ceasing production of bread crumbs in the absence of catastrophic losses that would result in the end of the seller's entire business.

b. **Reasonable Price.** Under UCC 2-305, when the price is not agreed upon the court will set a reasonable price as long as the parties intended to make a contract despite absence of agreement on price.

c. **Reasonable Time for Performance.** Under UCC 2-309 when the time for performance has not been agreed upon the goods must be shipped or delivered and payment must be made within a reasonable time.

1) **Price due at time of delivery.** Absent an agreement to the contrary, the price must be paid at the time of delivery of the goods. Payment of the price is a condition of the seller's duty to tender delivery of the goods and seller's tender of delivery is a condition of the buyer's duty to pay the price.

d. **Indefinite Duration.** Under UCC 2-309 when a contract for the sale of goods is for an indefinite duration or subject to termination by one or both of the parties, the duration of the contract is a reasonable time, but may be terminated at any time by either party, unless otherwise agreed.

e. **Unstated Time and Place for Payment.** Under UCC 2-310 the time and place for payment, in the absence of agreement, is at the time and place the buyer is to receive the goods.

4. **Indefinite Duration of Employment Contracts**. Employment contracts are terminable at the will of either party at any time unless the contract specifies otherwise. Courts may imply a minimum duration if pay or other terms are expressed with reference to a particular time.

Example: "$50,000 per year" may imply a minimum duration of a year; but "$20 per hour" may imply termination at any hour.

5. **Contracts For The Sale of an Interest in Real Estate.** To be enforceable a contract for the sale of real estate must identify the parcel with reasonable certainty; for specific performance it must be identified with precision. The price must also be definite. In

general, greater certainty is required in contracts for the sale of real estate than in other contracts. Further, the standard of definiteness for specific performance of real estate contracts is higher than if the remedy sought is limited to money damages.

6. **Restitution for Partial Performance of an Indefinite Agreement.** Where a contract fails due to indefiniteness, following part performance, the court will find a quasi-contract and award restitution to compensate for any benefit conferred by part performance.

7. **Agreements to Agree**. Where there is a contract on terms to be agreed upon or determined at a later date, the existence of a contract depends on the intent of the parties to be bound. Where the parties intended not to be bound, without an agreement on the undecided terms, there is no contract. However, where the parties manifested their intent to be bound, despite the absence of a term, there is a contract, with the undecided terms to be determined by the court according to reasonable standards.

   a. Where a term is to be determined by one of the parties, it must be set reasonably. If that party does not set the term, the other party may cancel the contract or set the term reasonably himself.

   b. Where the term is to be set by a third party, and the third party fails to set the term, the term shall be set reasonably by the court.

III. CONSIDERATION

A. CONSIDERATION OR PROMISSORY ESTOPPEL REQUIRED

In order to be enforceable, contracts must be supported by consideration, or there must be reasonable reliance on the promise. Promises to make a gift, where there is no reasonable reliance on the promise, are not enforceable.

1. **Bargain Theory of Consideration.** Consideration consists of a "bargained-for" exchange, usually consisting of a detriment or other change in position by each party in exchange for the promise of the other.

2. **Reciprocal Inducement**. To constitute consideration there must be a detriment; the promise must induce the detriment; and the detriment must be the inducement for the promise.

   Example: Betty promised to pay Sam $7,000 for his car with Sam promising to deliver the car for the $7,000 cash. Betty's promise to pay the $7,000 is a detriment. Her detriment was induced by Sam's promise to deliver the car. And, Sam's promise was the inducement for Betty's incurring the detriment of paying the $7,000. Likewise, delivery of the car by Sam is a detriment. His detriment was induced by Betty's promise to deliver the car. And, Betty's promise was the inducement for Sam's incurring the detriment of delivering the car. Thus, there is reciprocal inducement for each promise and consideration is present.

3. **Legal Detriment to the Promisee.** The detriment given in exchange for the promise may be any change in position by the promisee even if the thing given up is somehow beneficial to the person who incurs the detriment. So long as some legal right is given up the court will not inquire into whether the thing given up was beneficial or detrimental in some normative sense.

   Example: Uncle's promise to pay $5,000 if his niece "quits smoking" is enforceable where the niece quits smoking. Because the niece had a choice whether to quit smoking, her quitting is a legal detriment even though quitting smoking is generally regarded as healthy and beneficial.

4. **Promise as Consideration**. A return promise, given in exchange for a promise constitutes consideration. A promise, given in exchange for a return promise is consideration, so long as each promise, if performed, would constitute a legal detriment.

   Example: Builder promises to construct a home for Owner in exchange for Owner's promise to pay Builder $120,000. Because performance of each party's promise would constitute a legal detriment, each party's promise to perform is consideration for the promise of the other.

   a. **Failure of Consideration Distinguished.** Failure of consideration is used to refer to a breach by one of the parties. When one party fails to perform its side of the bargain, in breach of its promise, it is sometimes said that there has been a "failure of consideration." This does not mean that the contract is unenforceable due to an "absence of consideration." The parties' exchange of promises provided the necessary "consideration" and the contract is enforceable by the innocent party.

      Example: Seller promises to sell his auto to Buyer and Buyer, in exchange, promises to pay Seller the price of $1,500. Seller fails to deliver the car. There has been a "failure" of consideration. The parties' exchange of promises supplied the necessary element of consideration to make the agreement enforceable. The seller's failure to perform the consideration he agreed upon, delivery of the car, is nothing more than a breach, entitling buyer to damages.

MBE Advice

On the MBE, watch out for answer choices that say that a contract is invalid because of lack of consideration. Remember, ***any*** promise to do something you are not legally obligated to do is valid consideration, no matter how trivial. Since it does not take much to constitute valid consideration for a contract, consideration is rarely missing from a fact pattern.

B. GRATUITOUS OR GIFT PROMISES

A promise to make a gift is not supported by consideration and is not enforceable. The promisee incurs no detriment in exchange for the promise, and thus there is no consideration.

Example: An Aunt, upon learning that her nephew is attending college, promises to pay the nephew $5,000. Although the nephew's attendance at college may be the reason the promise was made, attending college was not induced by the promise; it is therefore not a detriment incurred in exchange for the promise and there is no consideration.

1. **Conditional Gift Not Supported By Consideration.** The fact that a promise to make a gift is subject to a condition does not mean that there is consideration. Performance of the condition is consideration for the promise only if the promise and the performance of the condition were **in exchange for one another.** If performance of the condition does not benefit the promisor in any way, the condition is not likely to have been part of an exchange or bargain.

   Example: "I'll give you a ride, if you meet me at the corner" is a promise to make a gift of a ride. The detriment of meeting the driver at the corner was not the inducement for the promise; there is no exchange and thus no consideration. The promise is not enforceable.

2. **Promise To Make Conditional Gift Supported by Consideration.** If, on the other hand, the performance of the condition was sought by the promisor, in exchange for the promise, there is consideration and the promise is enforceable. If the occurrence or performance of the condition confers a benefit on the promisor, it is likely that it was sought in exchange for the promise. Because of this, consideration is sometimes said to consist of either a "bargained-for detriment" or a "bargained-for benefit." If there is a "benefit to the promisor" in exchange for the promise, there is consideration.

   Example: Rich Uncle promises to pay Nephew $5,000 if Nephew abstains from drinking, smoking, and playing cards or billiards for money, until he is 21 years old. Abstinence from the vices is a legal detriment that was sought by Uncle in exchange for his promise. Any benefit to Uncle may be hard to discern and is not required so long as the detriment was sought in exchange for Uncle's promise. There is consideration in this famous case.

   Example: Wealthy Parishioner promises to pay $10,000 to his church, if the church names the parish library after him. The promise is supported by the consideration of naming the parish library in his honor. The condition of the gift was explicitly sought by the Wealthy Parishioner. It will also benefit him by creating a legacy in his name. The presence of this benefit helps show that the condition was sought in exchange for the promise.

3. **Promise To Make Gift to Charity.** A promise to make a gift to an organized charity, sometimes called a **charitable subscription** is enforceable, even in the absence of a

traditional exchange. Consideration is sometimes said to exist because of the promise of other donors who have participated in the fund drive or other effort to obtain promises to make gifts to the charity. Consideration is sometimes found in the implied promise of the charity to use the gift for the normal charitable purposes for which the charity was organized, or for some specific purpose mentioned by the donor or described in solicitations made by the charity. Other courts have simply ruled that promises to charities are enforceable even in the absence of consideration.

Example: Enormous State University solicited contributions to support programs for students seeking a career in chemistry. Wealthy Alumnus promised to donate $50,000 to the general fund of the University. The promise is supported by consideration based either on the promises of other donors to make similar contributions or on an implied promise by the University to maintain its program for students wishing to pursue a career in chemistry.

C. ADEQUACY OF CONSIDERATION

Courts **will not inquire** into the adequacy of the consideration or the comparability of the values exchanged. Where the element of a bargained-for exchange is present, the equivalence of the values will usually not be examined. Thus, a bargain to sell goods for an unusually low price, below the market value, will not be challenged as lacking in consideration. Despite this, a vast disparity in the values exchanged may be evaluated for any **unconscionability**, particularly if the contract was made in circumstances which indicated an absence of meaningful choice or "procedural" unconscionability, but the court will not characterize its inquiry as an investigation of the adequacy of consideration.

1. **Peppercorn Theory of Consideration.** An exchange of valuable real estate for nothing more than a "peppercorn" is enforceable so long as there is a real exchange. The relative market values involved will not invalidate the bargain. It is sometimes said that any consideration, "a horse, a hawk, or a robe," will be sufficient.

2. **Nominal or Sham Consideration.** An imbalance in the values exchanged, such as where valuable real estate is sold for "$1.00" may be evidence of a gift, misrepresentation, duress, mental incapacity, or unconscionability in the transaction. The Restatement 2d § 71 requires a real bargain and not merely the pretense of an exchange.

   Example: Uncle Roy promised to convey his farm and all its contents to Regina, his favorite niece, in exchange for $5, which Regina paid. The nominal consideration of $5 indicates that Uncle Roy may suffer from mental incapacity, or that Regina could only have reasonably understood his proposal as a joke, or that this was intended as a gift and not a real exchange of the farm for $5.

D. BARGAIN

Consideration requires a quid pro quo – a bargain in fact. Consideration is present only when the detriment to the promisee is given in exchange for the promise of the promisor. If the detriment is incurred before the promise is made, it cannot be incurred in exchange for the promise; likewise, if there is a pre-existing duty to incur the detriment, the detriment is not induced by the promise, and there is no consideration.

1. **Relinquishment of an Invalid Claim**, as in a settlement agreement, is consideration if the person giving up the right to sue does so with a good faith belief in the validity of the claim. Some courts require that the claim have some reasonable basis in law or fact.

   a. **Valid Claim.** Relinquishment of a valid claim is unquestionably consideration. Forbearance from suit on a valid claim, in exchange for a promise of payment of money or some other performance, is consideration.

   b. **Good Faith Belief in Invalid Claim.** Giving up an invalid claim, in exchange for a promise of payment, is consideration, and the promise of payment is enforceable, if the promisee had a good faith belief in the validity of the claim.

      1) Some courts also require that the claim have some reasonable basis in law or fact.

      Example: In exchange for Dave's promise to pay $50,000 to Linda, Linda agreed not to bring a paternity suit against Dave. A later blood test revealed that Dave was not the father of Linda's child; however, because Dave and Linda had engaged in sexual relations with one another, it was possible that Dave was the father, and Linda in good faith believed that he was. Because Linda had a good faith belief that Dave was the father, and had evidence to believe that he was, her agreement to give up her claim against him is consideration for his promise, even though her claim, if pursued, would eventually have failed.

2. **Pre-Existing Duty**. If the promisee has a pre-existing legal duty to incur the detriment, then performance of that duty is **not** consideration for a new promise.

   Example: Gem Jewelers offers a reward for the arrest of the gunman who robbed diamonds from its store. Alan is a police officer in the city where Gem Jewelers is located and captures the culprit. Alan has a pre-existing duty to arrest criminals in his jurisdiction and there is thus no consideration for Gem Jeweler's promise to pay him the reward.

   a. **Modification of Contracts**. The pre-existing duty rule makes one-sided modifications to contracts unenforceable. However, where each party's obligations are altered, there is a bargain and the modification is enforceable.

   Example: Landlord's agreement to reduce monthly rent due under a year-long lease is unenforceable absent some change in the Tenant's obligations. If the Tenant agrees to pay the smaller amount one day early each month, however, there is consideration for the modification – the landlord's promise to lease the premises for lower rent was made in exchange for the tenant's promise to make payment a day earlier.

1) **Consideration unnecessary for modification of contract for the sale of goods.** Under UCC 2-209, a **good faith modification** of contract for the sale of goods needs no consideration to be binding.

   Example: Seller's promise to accept a lower price than that previously agreed, in contract for the sale of goods, is enforceable despite absence of a new detriment given by the buyer.

   Example: Seller agreed to specially manufacture goods to buyer's specifications. Because the goods contain the Buyer's trademarked "logo," they are not suitable for sale to others. After Seller has completed manufacture, Buyer refuses to pay the price unless Seller, who will be financially ruined if Buyer does not make prompt payment, agrees to a reduction in the price. Seller reluctantly agrees. The modification to the price was not demanded in good faith and is not enforceable.

b. **Pre-existing Duty to a Third Person**. In some jurisdictions, a pre-existing duty by the promisee to a third-person does not make a promise unenforceable due to lack of consideration.

   Example: Jockey is hired to ride a thoroughbred in the Derby. Gambler promises Jockey a $1,000 bonus if the Jockey "wins." Although Jockey has a pre-existing duty to the owner of the horse, to ride to win, the promise is enforceable.

c. **Unanticipated Circumstances**. Where a contract is modified in response to an unanticipated change in circumstances, the modification is enforceable even though there is no change in the legal obligation of the promisee. It is **not necessary** that the change in circumstances was serious enough to excuse the other party from performance under the doctrine of impossibility, impracticability, or frustration.

   Example: Excavator Sub-Contractor has a contract with General Contractor to dig in land to prepare for pouring a foundation for a new building for a price of $30,000. Despite careful testing before the contract was made, debris was discovered underground, once work began, making the work far more difficult than expected. Excavator demanded $5,000 additional compensation for the work and General Contractor agreed. The promise of the additional payment is enforceable because of the unforeseen circumstances of the underground debris.

d. **Accord and Satisfaction**. The traditional common law rule is that payment of a sum smaller than an amount already owing is not consideration for a promise to forbear from suing for the larger amount; the debtor already had a pre-existing duty to pay the amount involved. However, a good faith dispute about the amount owing; payment at an earlier date; or modification due to unanticipated circumstances will provide the necessary additional detriment. In most jurisdictions, payment of a lesser sum in satisfaction of an undisputed obligation to pay a larger amount is effective as an accord and satisfaction.

3. **Illusory and Voidable Promises**. Agreements in which one party reserves too much discretion in determining the extent of his own performance, or in terminating or canceling the contract were traditionally treated as lacking consideration. The modern trend imposes an obligation of good faith or reasonableness which sufficiently restricts discretion and makes the contract enforceable.

   a. **Illusory Promises as Consideration.** An "illusory" promise is one involving the retention of unlimited discretion whether to perform, where the promise is little more than a commitment to "perform if I want."

      1) **Traditional Rule.** The traditional rule holds that no consideration is present where one party's obligation is illusory due to the retention of discretion whether to perform.

      2) **Modern Trend.** The promisor who retains discretion has an **implied duty of good faith and fair dealing** in the exercise of discretion. This implied duty supplies the necessary consideration.

      Example: Buyer agrees to purchase Blackacre if Buyer is able to obtain a mortgage loan for $100,000. The traditional rule would have held the contract unenforceable because of the Buyer's discretion over whether to apply for the loan. The modern rule imposes a duty of good faith, requiring the Buyer to make a good faith effort to obtain the loan, thus making the contract enforceable.

   b. **Consideration in Requirements and Output Contracts.** Under UCC 2-306, a contract for the sale of goods with the quantity measured by the buyer's requirements or the seller's output is **not unenforceable** due to a lack of consideration, even though one of the parties retains considerable discretion in determining the extent of its requirements or output. A contract which measures quantity by output of the seller or the requirements of the buyer means the actual output or requirements as may occur in **good faith.**

      1) Quantity may not be **unreasonably disproportionate** to any stated estimates or, if there is not a stated estimate, to any normal or otherwise comparable prior output or requirements.

      2) Buyer or Seller may not terminate the contract by shutting down its operations, unless doing so is necessary in good faith to avoid a catastrophic financial loss that would result in the failure of the entire business.

   c. **Exclusive Dealing Contracts.** UCC 2-306 provides that in an exclusive dealing contract, such as where the seller promises to provide the buyer with the exclusive right to sell or market the seller's goods, the buyer has **an implied obligation to use its best efforts** to sell or promote the distribution of the seller's merchandise.

Example: Wood enters into an agreement to have the exclusive right, within a specific geographic territory, to sell and distribute goods bearing Duff-Gordon's trademark. The agreement is not illusory because Wood has an implied duty to use his best efforts to market the goods.

d. **Termination or Cancellation by a Party.** A contract which gives one party the right to give notice terminating or canceling the contract at any time gives one party so much discretion that it might be "illusory."

1) **Termination "On Notice."** Where the contract requires "30 days" notice, or otherwise indicates a time for notice before termination, the contract is enforceable and is **not illusory**. The contract is treated as providing for alternative performances: "giving notice, or performing."

Example: Franchise agreement permitting the franchisor to terminate the franchise at any time, upon 2 weeks notice, is not illusory.

2) Where there is no specific time indicated for advance notice of termination, some cases still conclude that there is no consideration because of the illusory nature of the obligation to perform. Some modern cases hold that an obligation to "give notice" may supply the necessary consideration.

3) **Termination of Contracts for Sale of Goods.** In contracts for the sale of goods, UCC 2-309 provides that a clause permitting "termination by one party" **requires reasonable notification** that is actually received by the other party and an agreement permitting termination without reasonable notification is unconscionable. If notification is not required, or if the time for notification is unreasonable and thus unconscionable, the contract may still be terminated but reasonable notification must be given.

Example: Gas station lease permitting landlord to terminate at any time, with notice, is an unenforceable illusory contract. Modern cases and UCC 2-309 would rule that the fact that notice is required renders the contract enforceable.

Example: Gasoline distribution agreement, permitting Seller to terminate at any time, upon notice to the Buyer, is an enforceable contract, but UCC 2-309 requires that notice be reasonable.

4) **Termination Upon the Occurrence of a Specific Event**. A contract terminable in the discretion of one party, but only on the occurrence of a specific event, beyond the control of the person exercising the discretion, is not illusory.

Example: A contract providing that Seller may terminate the contract if the market price of the goods involved in the contract exceeds a predetermined price is not illusory because the Seller has no control over the market price.

E. CONTRACTS WITHOUT CONSIDERATION

Substitutes for Consideration. Agreements are sometimes enforceable in the absence of consideration. These situations include a contract enforceable under the seal, past or "moral" consideration, contract modifications under UCC 2-209, and promissory estoppel (Detrimental Reliance on a promise).

1. **The Seal**. At common law a "seal" made promises enforceable in the absence of consideration under **writ of Covenant.** It traditionally consisted of the use of an imprint on melted candle wax and later consisted of nothing more than a pre-printed "S" on a pre-printed contract.

Essay Advice

For states that also test Contracts in essay form

For purposes of state bar examinations that test Contracts in essay form, under state law the seal is no longer effective in most states.

2. **Past or "Moral" Consideration**. A promise made to pay a moral obligation or to pay a previously discharged legal obligation is not supported by consideration but may be enforceable where the moral obligation is based on the receipt of a valuable benefit or where the legal obligation was discharged by operation of law, as in expiration of the statute of limitations or discharge in bankruptcy.

   a. **Promise To Pay a Debt Discharged By Operation of Law.** Sometimes a person makes a renewed promise to pay an old debt that, due to the operation of some law, is no longer enforceable. The question is whether this new promise is enforceable in the absence of any new consideration from the promisee. Even though there is nothing given in exchange, a new promise to pay a debt or other obligation discharged by operation of law is enforceable on the basis of **Moral Consideration**. These new promises are enforceable where the original debt was made unenforceable due to the following:

      1) **Discharge in Bankruptcy.** When a debt is discharged in bankruptcy, the debtor sometimes makes a new promise to pay the discharged debt. **Moral Consideration** makes these promises enforceable under contract law. However, enforceability of the promise to pay the discharged debt is limited by Bankruptcy Code § 524. Such agreements are called **"reaffirmation agreements**." They now

require a written agreement, entered into after discharge by the bankruptcy court. The agreement must be subject to a right of rescission for 60 days, and is enforceable only if accompanied by the debtors' attorney's affidavit that the "reaffirmation" will not impose an undue hardship on the debtor or the debtor's dependants. If the reaffirmation agreement is not accompanied by an attorney's affidavit, the agreement must be approved by the court as not imposing an undue hardship and as being in the best interest of the debtor.

2) **Expiration of the Statute of Limitations.** A promise to pay a debt previously discharged by the statute of limitations is enforceable, even though there is no new consideration given in exchange for the new promise.

Example: Debtor borrowed $10,000 from Creditor, but the obligation became unenforceable due to expiration of the statute of limitations. After expiration of the statute of limitations, Debtor made a new promise to pay the $10,000. The new promise to pay is enforceable, even though there is no new consideration for the promise.

3) **Incapacity, such as "Infancy."** A promise, upon reaching the age of majority, to perform the contract made during infancy, is enforceable even though there is no new consideration given in exchange for the renewed promise.

4) **Fraud**. A promise to perform an obligation, originally unenforceable due to fraud, is enforceable without consideration for the renewed promise.

b. **Previously Conferred Substantial Benefit.** A promise made in recognition of a previously conferred benefit, of substantial value, may be enforceable. Because the promise was made only after the benefit was conferred, there is not a "bargained-for exchange" traditionally required as consideration. Despite this, courts have enforced these promises holding that consideration was present. To be enforceable there must have been a direct and substantial benefit to the promisor. Benefits conferred upon a third party do not suffice.

Example: Over a period of many years a widow provided meals, transportation, and other care to an elderly millionaire in the years prior to his death. He gave her a promissory note for $25,000 in recognition of her services. The promise is enforceable even though the promise was not given "in exchange" for the benefit.

Example: Stranger took care of a young adult when he was injured while far away from home, paying for his medical care, food, and shelter. Upon learning of the care provided to his son, Father promised to reimburse the Stranger for his help. The promise is not enforceable because Father received no direct benefit from the services provided by the Stranger.

3. **Modification of a Contract**. One-sided modifications of an existing contract were traditionally not enforceable because of the absence of consideration. The modern trend is to enforce good faith modifications, even in the absence of consideration.

   a. **Minor Change as Consideration for Modification.** Consideration exists for an agreed modification where there is any change of the promisee's rights or duties, no matter how small or trivial. For example, consideration would exist where Landlord agrees to accept a lower rent, in exchange for Tenant's promise to make rental payments one day earlier than required by the original lease.

   b. **Unanticipated Change of Circumstances.** Consideration is present where the modification is made in light of unanticipated or changed circumstances.

   c. **Good Faith Modification of Contracts for Sale of Goods.** UCC 2-209 permits enforcement of modifications of contracts for the sale of goods, without consideration, so long as the modification is made in good faith.

4. **Promissory Estoppel (Detrimental Reliance).** A promise is enforceable, without consideration, where the promisee **actually acted in reliance** on the promise and the promisor should reasonably have expected reliance to occur; however, the remedy may be limited as justice requires.

> ***Watch Out!***
>
> Lack of an otherwise enforceable agreement is a requirement for promissory estoppel. Where an enforceable contract exists, there cannot be promissory estoppel.

   a. **Actual Reliance.** For a promise to be enforceable based on promissory estoppel, the promisee must actually rely on the promise to his detriment. Action taken by the promisee must have been induced by the promise and not constitute action that the promisee would have undertaken regardless of the promise.

   Example: An employer's promise of a pension to an employee, upon the employee's announcement of her retirement, is not enforceable, where the employee would have retired anyway. However, if the employee retired *only* in reliance on the employer's promise of a pension, this element is satisfied.

   b. **Reliance Foreseeable.** In addition, the promisor must have **reasonably expected the promisee to rely** on the promise to his detriment. The reliance must be reasonably foreseeable.

Example: Grandfather promises to pay his Granddaughter $2,000, expressing the hope that the money will make it possible for her to quit working. Foreseeability of her action in quitting her job makes the promise enforceable.

c. **Remedy May Be Limited as Justice Requires**. A promise enforceable under promissory estoppel may not be completely enforceable, via specific performance, or expectation damages, but may only be enforceable to the extent of the promisee's reliance expense.

MBE Advice

On the MBE, be somewhat skeptical of answer choices that are based upon *detrimental reliance* or *promissory estoppel.* The bar examiners are interested in testing your knowledge of the mechanics of contract formation. However, *detrimental reliance* and *promissory estoppel* are equitable rules designed to avoid the technicalities of contract formation. These answer choices are enticing because they seem to provide an easy way to ensure a just result. But it is precisely for that reason that they are often traps on the MBE.

IV. STATUTE OF FRAUDS

The "Statute of Frauds" refers to any statutory requirement that a particular type of contract must be in writing in order to be enforceable. It also refers specifically to the traditional statute of frauds enacted in 17th century England and reproduced in every state's statutes.

Watch Out!

Even when the parties seem to have a valid contract with an offer, acceptance, and consideration, keep in mind that the *Statute of Frauds* may make that contract unenforceable.

A. TYPES OF CONTRACTS "WITHIN" THE STATUTE OF FRAUDS

A contract required to be in writing in order to be enforceable is said to be "within" the statute of frauds.

1. **Executor's Promise To Pay from His Own Estate**. A personal promise by the executor of an estate to pay the estate's debts from the executor's own assets must be in writing.

2. **A Promise To Answer for the Debt of Another**. A promise by a person to guarantee the debt of another must be in writing. This frequently occurs when parents guarantee the debt of a child, or when a corporate officer guarantees the obligation of his corporation. This should be distinguished from situations where a person makes a contract to benefit a third person.

   Example: Nephew enters into contract with Auto Dealer for purchase of car, on credit. Uncle promises to pay for car if Nephew defaults. Uncle's promise is to pay for the debt of another and must be in writing to be enforceable, under the statute of frauds.

   Example: Mother purchases car for Son, promising Auto Dealer that she will pay for the car. Because Mother is purchasing the car, this is not a contract to pay the Son's debt. Son has no debt.

3. **Contracts in Consideration of Marriage**. Any contract where "marriage" is the consideration, other than mutual promises to marry, must be in writing. Pre-nuptial contracts where "marriage" is the consideration are "within" the statute, but contracts in contemplation of marriage, where the marriage itself is not part of the consideration for the contract, are not within the statute.

4. **Contracts for the Transfer of Interest in Real Estate**. Any contract for the transfer of an interest in real estate, whether for the purchase or sale of real estate, a lease of real estate, or to convey a mortgage on real estate must be in writing. Any interest in real estate will trigger the statute, whether it is a fee interest, a mere leasehold, or an easement. A mere "license," however, is not generally regarded as an interest in real estate and thus need not be in writing under the traditional statute of frauds.

5. **Contracts Not Capable of Being Performed Within a Year of Their Making**. Any contract which 'by its terms' cannot be performed within a year of its making must be in writing. A contract which is likely to take more than a year to perform, but where performance is permitted to take less than a year, is not within the statute.

   Example: A contract to provide nursing care "for the rest of the patient's life" is **not within** the statute, even though the patient is young with a life expectancy of over a year. The contract could conceivably be performed within a year.

   Example: A contract for employment for 8 months, with performance to begin in 5 months from the time the contract is made, however, is within the statute because performance cannot be completed within a year (8 months plus 5 months) of its making.

6. **Contracts for Sale of Goods With Price of $500 or More Under UCC 2-201.** A contract for sale of goods for a price of $500 or more must be in writing. A contract for the sale of goods of $499 is not within the statute. A contract with a price of precisely $500 is within the statute and must be in writing. The fact that the **value** of the goods is greater or less than $500 does not matter; the **actual contract price determines** whether the statute applies.

7. **Lease of Goods for Rent of $1,000 or More.** Under UCC 2A-201 an agreement for the lease of goods, such as an equipment lease, or car rental contract, for a total rent of $1,000 or more must be in writing to be enforceable.

8. **Other Personal Property Worth More Than $5,000.** Under UCC 1-206, a contract for the transfer of personal property (other than *goods* which are governed by UCC 2-201) for an amount or value of **more than** $5,000 must be in writing. The writing must: 1) indicate that a contract for sale has been made between the parties; 2) at a defined or stated price; 3) reasonably identify the subject matter of the sale; and 4) be signed by the party against whom enforcement is sought. If the contract is an agreement for the sale or lease of goods, the statute of frauds provision of UCC 2-201 (for sales) or 2A-201 (for leases) governs instead.

   Example: Writer and Publisher enter into an oral contract for transfer of Writer's right to receive royalties from his book, for a price of $7,000. The agreement is not enforceable unless there is a writing that meets the requirements of UCC 1-206.

   Example: Used Car Dealer and Customer make oral agreement for purchase of auto for price of $4,500. Because the contract is one for the sale of goods, UCC 2-201's $500 or more threshold governs, not the "more than $5,000" standard of UCC 1-206. The contract is not enforceable unless there is a sufficient writing or the statute is otherwise satisfied.

B. SUFFICIENCY OF THE WRITING

The writing containing the essential terms of the contract must be signed by the party against whom enforcement is sought.

1. **Form of the Writing.** The form of the writing does not matter. It may be a formal written contract, a letter, memorandum, or other writing. It may consist of a composite of several documents which, taken together, satisfy the statute.

2. **Signed by the Defendant.** The writing must be signed by the party against whom enforcement is sought. It is not necessary for both parties to sign.

   a. **Signature.** A signature may consist of a handwritten signature, an "X", or any symbol made with the intent to authenticate a writing. Under UCC 1-201, a signature may include the use of letter head stationary or pre-printed forms bearing the party's name or other symbol if the stationary or form was adopted with the **intent to authenticate.**

3. **Other Contents of the Writing**. In addition to the defendant's signature, the writing must indicate that a contract has been made and must contain the following elements:

   a. It must indicate the **identity of the parties;**

b. It must show that a contract between the parties has been made or offered by the person who signed;

c. The **subject matter of the contract**, including a reasonable description of any real estate involved;

d. The **agreed consideration** and other **essential terms**.

4. **Sufficiency of the Writing in Contracts for the Sale of Goods under UCC 2-201.** Article 2 of the UCC significantly relaxes the writing requirement. Under UCC 2-201(1) the writing must only contain a signature by the party against whom enforcement is sought, an indication that there is a contract for the sale of goods, and a quantity term.

   a. **Essential Terms not Required.** UCC 2-201. A writing is not insufficient because it omits essential terms or because it misstates terms, but the contract is not enforceable beyond the quantity term stated in the writing.

5. **Confirmatory Memorandum Exception in Contract for Sale of Goods "Between Merchants."** In a contract for the sale of goods the statute is satisfied "between merchants," if within a reasonable time a writing in confirmation of the contract, which is sufficient against the sender, is received, and the party receiving it has reason to know its contents, unless that party gives written notice of objection to its contents within 10 days of receipt. In this way the statute can be satisfied against a person who did not sign the writing, if he received it and failed to make a timely objection.

   a. **The Transaction Must Be "Between Merchants."**

      1) **Between Merchants as defined in UCC 2-104.** A transaction is "between merchants" when both parties are "merchants."

      2) **Merchant as defined in UCC 2-104.** A "Merchant" is a person who "deals in goods of the kind, or otherwise by his occupation holds himself out as having knowledge or skill peculiar to the practices or goods involved in the transaction." A person can also be a merchant if such knowledge or skill can be attributed to the person because of his employment as an agent, broker, or other intermediary, who by his occupation holds himself out as having such knowledge or skill.

   b. **Sufficient against the Sender.** The writing must be "sufficient against the sender." It must be "signed" by the sender, must indicate that a contract for sale has been made between the parties, and is not enforceable beyond the quantity stated in the writing.

   c. **Reason To Know Contents.** The person who received it must "have reason to know its contents."

   d. **Written Notice of Objection Within 10 Days.** The statute of frauds is satisfied under this provision only if the person who received it **did not** give notice of objection to its contents within 10 days after it is received. If the recipient gives timely written notice of objection, the statute is not satisfied against the recipient.

Example: Manufacturer made an oral agreement to sell 200,000 yards of carpet to Distributor for $500,000. The next day Manufacturer sent Distributor a signed confirmation of the transaction, describing the 200,000 yards of carpet, but failing to mention the price. Distributor received the letter but did not respond. The confirmatory memo sent by Manufacturer and received by Distributor satisfies the statute of frauds against both parties. It is signed by Manufacturer, demonstrates the existence of the contract, and contains a quantity term. The fact that the price is missing does not matter. It also satisfies the statute against Distributor, even though Distributor did not sign it. Both parties are merchants because as carpet manufacturer and carpet dealer they deal in goods of the kind. Distributor had reason to know of the contents based on the phone conversation and received the confirmation but failed to object in writing to its contents within 10 days of receipt.

e. **Satisfaction of Statute Does Not Prove Offer and Acceptance.** Satisfaction of the statute of frauds does not, by itself, satisfy the requirement that a contract be formed. The plaintiff, in addition to satisfying the statute of frauds, must demonstrate the elements of mutual assent and consideration.

C. PART PERFORMANCE TO SATISFY THE STATUTE OF FRAUDS

Part Performance satisfies the statute of frauds but only to the extent of the performance rendered. It does not make executory portions of the contract enforceable.

1. **Part Performance of Contracts Not Performable Within a Year.** Part performance does not satisfy the "one-year" provision of the statute, except to the extent that performance has actually been rendered.

   Example: Homeowner orally agrees to engage services of Gardner for 3 years at a price of $20,000 per year. Gardner works for 1 year. Gardner is entitled to be paid for the year's worth of work, but his part performance does not satisfy the statute with respect to the remaining 2 years.

2. **Part Performance: Goods Accepted or Paid for.** Under UCC 2-201(3) the statute of frauds is satisfied with respect to a contract for the sale of goods for which payment has been made and accepted, or where the goods have been received by the buyer and accepted by him.

   Example: Buyer and Seller entered into an oral agreement for delivery of 10,000 bricks at a price of $500 per 1000. Seller had delivered and Buyer accepted 3000 of the bricks when Buyer repudiated. The contract has been satisfied with respect to the 3000 bricks delivered and accepted by the buyer, but is not enforceable beyond that quantity absent a sufficient writing.

3. **Real Estate: Part Performance of a Land Sale Contract.** Where the buyer has taken possession and made substantial improvements on land, pursuant to a contract of sale, so that the performance is "unequivocally referable" to the contract, the statute has been satisfied.

4. **Part Performance: Specially Manufactured Goods.** Under UCC 2-201(3), a contract for the sale of goods is enforceable despite the absence of a signed writing where it is a contract for the sale of:

   a. **goods to be specially manufactured** for the buyer;

   b. the goods are **not suitable for sale to others** in the ordinary course of the seller's business; and

   c. before notice of the buyer's repudiation is received, the **seller has made a substantial beginning** of their manufacture, **or commitments** for their procurement.

D. EQUITABLE AND PROMISSORY ESTOPPEL TO SATISFY THE STATUTE OF FRAUDS

1. **Equitable Estoppel.** Misrepresentation of fact by a party, in asserting that no writing was necessary, will impose an equitable estoppel, preventing that party from asserting the statute of frauds as a defense.

   Example: Oral employment contract for 18 months. Employee asked to have contract in writing. Employer told Employee that employment contracts did not have to be in writing in order to be enforceable. Employer's misrepresentation will estop Employer from asserting the statute of frauds as a defense.

2. **Promissory Estoppel.** Traditional cases do not permit enforcement of a promise within the statute of frauds on the basis of detrimental reliance. However, some modern cases hold and Restatement 2d § 139 provides that a promise which the promisor should reasonably expect to induce action or forbearance is enforceable though not in writing where the promisee or a third party takes action or forbears in reliance on the promise.

   Example: Airline orally promised Pilot employment for 2 years. In reliance, Pilot left his employment with another airline. The promise is enforceable, despite the absence of a writing, due to the foreseeable reliance by the Pilot.

   Example: Farmers entered into oral contract for sale of grain to Elevator. In reliance, Elevator entered into a contract for resale of the promised grain. Promise is enforceable despite lack of benefit conferred on Farmer and absence of the Farmer's promise to execute any necessary writing.

a. **Recovery Limited To Reliance Expense.** Recovery may be limited to the value of the expense incurred in reliance on the promise or the value of any benefit conferred on the promisor as a result of the promise.

b. **Unjust Enrichment Sometimes Required.** Some courts adhere to the traditional rule refusing to enforce a promise, due to foreseeable reliance, absent unjust enrichment.

Example: Father promised Stepson "if you remain on the farm and work it with me, I will leave the farm to you on my death." In reliance on this promise, Stepson gave up other opportunities and remained on the farm, working it with his stepfather. Upon Father's death, promise was specifically enforceable, despite the absence of a writing for the transfer of an interest in the real estate, because of Stepson's reliance and unjust enrichment to Father that would otherwise result. The promise would be enforceable in a jurisdiction requiring both reliance and unjust enrichment.

3. **Estoppel By Admission in Contracts For Sale of Goods.** Under UCC 2-201(3), in a contract for the sale of goods the statute is satisfied if the party against whom enforcement is sought admits in his pleading, testimony, or otherwise in court, that a contract for sale was made. But, the contract is not enforceable beyond the quantity admitted.

E. MODIFICATIONS OF CONTRACTS REQUIRED TO BE IN WRITING

1. **Modification of Essential Terms of Contract within the Statute of Frauds.** If the contract is one "within" the statute of frauds, any modification of essential terms must be in writing.

2. **Modification of Contracts for Sale of Goods.** In a contract for the sale of goods, UCC 2-209 requires modifications to be in writing if the contract "as modified" is for a price of $500 or more.

3. **Contractual Provisions Requiring Written Modifications**. Written contracts sometimes contain terms requiring any modification to be made in writing. These provisions are generally enforceable in the absence of a waiver or estoppel. However, performance of oral modifications, such as in a construction contract where change orders are implemented for an additional price, will usually constitute a waiver of the requirement of a written modification in order to prevent unjust enrichment.

a. **"No Oral Modifications" Clause Enforceable Unless Waived.** Written contracts may provide that any subsequent modifications must be in writing in order to be enforceable. This "no oral modifications" clause will be enforceable, unless waived.

1) **Waiver by Conduct.** Conduct by the parties, manifesting waiver of the provision requiring modifications to be in writing, such as by performance of additional work pursuant to an oral modification, may result in the unenforceability of such a

clause. A "no oral modification" clause will not be enforced where to do so would result in unjust enrichment.

Example: A written contract between Builder and Homeowner requires any modification to be in a signed writing. During construction, Homeowner asked Builder to substitute copper pipe for the plastic pipe called for in the written contract. Builder installed the copper pipe. Homeowner's conduct in seeking the change and permitting it to be made, despite the absence of a written modification, will be treated as a waiver of the requirement of a written modification.

2) UCC 2-209 gives effect to "no oral modification" clauses in contracts for the sale of goods, but allows for their waiver, by conduct or otherwise.

b. **Parol Evidence Rule Irrelevant.** The Parol Evidence Rule does not affect oral modifications, made subsequent to the execution of a fully integrated written contract (see below on *Parol Evidence Rule*).

Watch Out!

If a contract is subject to the Statute of Frauds, it will not be enforceable unless it is **in writing**. When you encounter a question on the bar exam in which the enforceability of an *oral* contract is at issue, the first thing you must do is pull from memory a list of the kinds of contracts which are covered by the Statute of Frauds. If a particular contract is not covered by your list, it will be enforceable in spite of the fact that it is oral.

V. PAROL EVIDENCE RULE AND INTERPRETATION OF WRITTEN CONTRACTS

A. PAROL EVIDENCE RULE

1. **Evidence of Prior or Contemporaneous Agreements Excluded.** The Parol Evidence Rule prohibits the use of evidence of a prior or contemporaneous agreement to vary or contradict the terms of a written contract that the parties intended as a final and complete expression of their agreement.

a. **Integrated Writing.** The Parol Evidence Rule only governs when there is a partially or fully integrated written contract, intended by the parties as a final expression of their agreement. A writing not intended as final is not integrated and will not bar the introduction of evidence of contradictory terms.

b. **Role of the Court.** The judge will make an initial determination of whether a writing was intended as a partial or fully integrated written contract. In making this determination, the judge may consider the parol evidence. If the writing is not integrated, or, if it is only partially integrated and the parol evidence does not contradict the writing, the judge will permit the jury to consider the parol evidence to determine whether the offered evidence was part of the agreement between the parties.

c. **Evidence of Subsequent Modification Admissible.** The Parol Evidence Rule **does not** prohibit evidence of a subsequent modification of a written contract, but the contract might provide that such modifications must be in writing.

2. **Integrated Written Contract**. For the Parol Evidence Rule to apply there must be at least a partially integrated writing. Writings may be completely unintegrated, partially integrated, or fully integrated.

a. **Completely Unintegrated Writings** are writings that the parties did not intend to be final expressions of any part of their agreement.

b. **Partially Integrated Writings** are those intended as "final," but not complete, expressions of the terms they contain. They are final with respect to the terms included in the writing, but are not intended to constitute the exclusive statement of all of the terms of the agreement between the parties.

1) **Parol Evidence Permitted To Supplement But Not Contradict Partially Integrated Contract.** Parol evidence may be used to supplement, but not "contradict," the terms of a partially integrated writing. Consistency depends on whether there is a "direct contradiction" or, under a more restrictive view, an "absence of reasonable harmony" between the writing and parol term.

Example: Parol evidence was excluded from showing that a contract for sale of a quantity of scrap steel was subject to the parol condition that the Seller could obtain the steel from a particular agreed upon source. While the parol evidence did not "directly contradict" the writing, there was an absence of reasonable harmony between the unconditional writing and the proposed parol condition sought to be introduced.

2) **Evidence of a Course of Dealing, Usage of Trade, or Course of Performance** may also be used to explain or supplement a written sale of goods contract, whether partially integrated or fully integrated.

c. **Fully Integrated Written Contract May Not be Supplemented.** A fully integrated written contract is one intended as a final and complete expression of the agreement between the parties. A fully integrated contract is the exclusive statement of all of the terms of the contract and may not be supplemented with parol evidence.

1) **General Rule:** Parol evidence **may not** be used to supplement a fully integrated writing.

2) **Exception To Rule in Contracts for the sale of goods.** UCC 2-202 permits use of evidence of course of dealing, usage of trade, or course of performance to supplement an integrated writing. However, they may not contradict the written contract.

3. **Test for Complete or Partial Integration:** Intent of the parties determines whether a written agreement is unintegrated, partially integrated, or completely integrated.

a. **Four Corners Test.** The traditional test examines the "four corners" of the writing to determine if it appears to be a complete and final expression of the contract between the parties. Evidence extrinsic to the writing is not considered.

b. **Contextual Test.** Modern courts use a "contextual test" considering extrinsic evidence of the parties' intent, to determine whether there are circumstances that explain the omission of the term from the writing even though it was agreed upon and intended to be part of the agreement.

1) **Term Naturally Omitted From the Writing.** Restatement 2d § 216 asks whether the term might "naturally have been omitted" from the writing if it was part of the contract. If so, then the agreement will **not** be regarded as fully integrated.

2) **Certain Inclusion Test**. In contracts for the sale of goods, a more liberal test is used. It permits introduction of the evidence, treating the writing as a partial integration, **unless the term "certainly would have been included"** in the writing if it was meant to be part of the agreement between the parties.

c. **Effect of Merger Clause**. Written contracts sometimes include a clause indicating that "this writing is intended as a final and complete expression of the agreement between the parties," thus expressing the intent to "merge" all prior agreements into the single document.

1) **Four Corners Test:** Absent some obvious appearance on the face of the writing that it is incomplete, a merger clause resolves the question of intent that the writing is a complete integration of the contract.

2) **Contextual Test**: Merger clause is an important factor affecting the determination of integration, but other evidence regarding the circumstances surrounding the execution of the contract will be considered. Evidence of some unfairness or unconscionability in the creation of the contract may show that the contract was not intended as a complete integration despite the inclusion of the merger clause.

3) **Form Contracts.** Merger clauses in standardized form contracts are unenforceable by some courts where parol representations were made to induce one of the parties to enter into the contract without realizing that the exclusion from the agreement would render those parol promises unenforceable.

4. **Exceptions to Parol Evidence Rule**. Parol evidence will be admissible, despite the presence of an integrated writing in order to resolve an ambiguity, prove invalidity of the contract, to show mutual mistake or scrivener's error, to establish a parol condition precedent, or to establish the existence of a second or "collateral" agreement with separate consideration.

a. **Ambiguity** – Parol evidence will be admitted to resolve an ambiguity in the meaning of the written contract.

1) **Plain Meaning Test.** Traditional test determines "plain meaning" of the language to resolve any ambiguities, excluding evidence of prior negotiations to establish the existence of an ambiguity.

2) **Contextual Text.** Modern contextual test permits the use of extrinsic evidence, including evidence of prior negotiations or other circumstances, to establish the existence of an ambiguity so long as the writing is **"reasonably susceptible"** to the meaning suggested by the extrinsic evidence.

Example: Parol evidence was admitted to explain that language providing that Contractor would indemnify Owner "against all loss, damage, expense and liability resulting from injury or damage to property connected with the work" was intended to only refer to property of "third persons," and not to payment for loss for damage to the Owner's own property.

Example: Contract provided for sale of "chickens." Parol evidence of a usage of trade was introduced to clarify ambiguity over whether the contract called for tender "frying chickens" or permitted delivery of less desirable "stewing chickens."

b. **Invalid Contract**. Parol evidence is admissible to demonstrate that the contract is avoidable or unenforceable due to fraud, duress, or mutual mistake, or for damages for misrepresentation.

Example: Parol evidence of fraudulent misrepresentations about opportunity for Employee to acquire an ownership interest in the Employer's business was admissible in action to recover for fraud, based on false representations made to induce Employer to enter into written employment contract which was silent regarding the Employee's right to become a part owner.

c. **Mutual Mistake**. Parol evidence is admissible to demonstrate that the contract was entered pursuant to a "mutual mistake."

d. **Reformation due to Mutual Mistake or "Scrivener's Error."** Parol evidence is admissible to show that there was a mistake in the "expression" of the agreement, and that the parties executed the integrated agreement pursuant to a "mutual mistake" that it accurately represented the terms of their agreement.

Example: Parol evidence was admissible to reform a written deed, mistakenly containing a legal description of all of Blackacre where the agreement of the parties was for the conveyance of only a portion of the parcel.

e. **Conditional Formation. Condition Precedent to Contract Formation.** Parol evidence can be admitted to demonstrate that, despite the existence of a writing, there was an unexpressed condition to the creation of the contract. To be admissible, the evidence must show that there was a condition precedent to the enforceability of the contract, and not simply a condition subsequent which would discharge the duties created by the contract.

Example: Al, Bill, and Charlie, three out of four brothers who jointly own stock in A-Z Corp. execute a written contract guaranteeing a debt owed by A-Z Corp. Unexpressed in the agreement is the understanding that Al, Bill, and Charlie's obligation is conditional on obtaining the joint guarantee of their fourth brother, Dave. Evidence of the condition precedent is admissible.

f. **Collateral Agreement.** Evidence can be introduced to show the existence of a second or "collateral agreement." Parol Evidence of a separate agreement is admissible where the collateral agreement relates to separate subject matter for which independent consideration was provided. Where the subject matter of the collateral agreement is so closely related to the subject of the fully integrated written contract so that it would naturally have been included in the written contract, and there is no separate consideration for the second agreement, the evidence is excluded. It might be included to supplement a partially integrated agreement, if it is not contradictory.

Example: Evidence of a promise to tear down an ugly shed on adjacent property was excluded where there was an apparently fully integrated written contract for the sale of a mansion and no separate consideration, apart from payment for the mansion, for removal of the shed.

Example: Evidence of a contract to deliver several lectures, for additional compensation, should be admitted as evidence of a collateral contract, despite the existence of an integrated written contract for the production of a written work, for a fee, on the same topics as those to be covered in the lectures. There are two separate contracts, one written and one oral, each with separate consideration

B. EFFECT OF USAGE OF TRADE, COURSE OF DEALING, AND COURSE OF PERFORMANCE

1. **Agreement Defined.** Under UCC 1-201 the terms of an "agreement" consist of the "bargain of the parties in fact" as found in their language, by implication from circumstances surrounding the making of the agreement, and from any usage of trade, course of dealing, or course of performance applicable to the transaction.

2. **Usage of Trade.** Under UCC 1-205, a usage of trade is "any practice or method of dealing having such regularity of observance in a place, vocation, or trade as to justify an expectation that it will be observed with respect to the transaction in question. A usage of trade is an **industry or local custom**.

3. **Course of Dealing.** Under UCC 1-205, a course of dealing is a "**sequence of previous conduct between the parties** to a particular transaction which is fairly to be regarded as establishing a common basis of understanding for interpreting their expressions and other conduct." A course of dealing is a customary practice between the parties to a transaction based on their prior dealings with one another. Where a course of dealing conflicts with a usage of trade, the course of dealing controls.

4. **Course of Performance.** Under UCC 2-208, a course of performance may develop where a particular contract for sale involves **repeated occasions for performance** by either party with knowledge of the nature of the performance and an opportunity for objection by the other. Any course of performance accepted or acquiesced in without objection is relevant to the meaning of the agreement.

5. **Priority of Terms**: Express Agreements, Usage of Trade, Course of Dealing, and Course of Performance.

    a. **Consistent Interpretation where Possible.** When possible the express terms of the agreement and any trade usage, or course of dealing or performance should be construed as consistent with one another, unless consistent construction is unreasonable.

    b. **Express Terms Control.** Express terms of the agreement control any trade usage, course of dealing, or course of performance, except that course of performance may operate as a modification or waiver of an express term.

    c. **Course of Performance Controls Course of Dealing or Trade Usage**.

    d. **Course of Dealing Controls Usage of Trade**.

C. INTERPRETATION

Contracts should be interpreted according to their reasonable meaning in light of the language used by the parties, the circumstances surrounding the making of the contract, applicable customary meanings and usage of trade as well as any course of dealing and course of performance between the parties.

1. **General Rules of Interpretation**:

    a. **Construe Ambiguities Against the Draftsman**. Ambiguities are generally interpreted against the person who drafted the provision in question. This is particularly true in situations involving standardized form contracts.

    b. **Expression of One Thing Excludes the Other.** The expression of one thing is the exclusion of the other (from the Latin phrase "Expressio Unius Est Exclusio Alterius"). When the parties provide a list of included items, without general language indicating that the list is merely illustrative and not meant to be exclusive, the inclusion of items on the list implies the exclusion of unmentioned items. However, where a general or inclusive term is used, the list will be treated as merely illustrative.

    Example: Language in a contract for the sale of a house indicating that the sale of the house will include "washer, dryer, refrigerator and range" will be interpreted to exclude the "dishwasher." However, language indicating that the sale will cover the "washer, dryer, refrigerator, range, and other kitchen appliances" will be likely interpreted to refer to other similar items, such as the dishwasher and built-in microwave oven.

    c. **Conflicting Language** – should be construed, where possible, in a manner which permits every portion of the agreement to have meaning.

        1) **Specific Terms Govern over General.** Where language in a contract conflicts, specific terms should control general terms.

        2) **Bargained Terms Prevail.** Terms specifically negotiated prevail over boilerplate or other terms not bargained over.

2. **Interpretation Favoring Fairness and the Public Interest**. Where language is reasonably susceptible of two meanings, it should be interpreted in accord with the meaning that is more compatible with fairness and the public interest.

VI. PERFORMANCE AND BREACH

A. CONDITIONS

Contractual duties are frequently subject to conditions that must occur before the obligation created by the contract becomes due. A condition is an event, uncertain to occur, upon which a duty to perform depends.

1. **Interpretation of Conditions.** The meaning of conditions depends upon the intent of the parties.

   a. **Conditions Distinguished from Promises.** Terms in contracts may be interpreted as either promises or conditions.

      1) **Promises.** Promises create a duty to perform. Failure to perform a promise gives rise to a right to damages for breach of the promise, particularly where the failure to perform is nothing more than a minor breach. Failure to perform a promise may constitute a minor or a material breach. The duty to perform a promise may be made subject to a condition.

      2) **Conditions.** Conditions are events which if they occur, either trigger the imposition of a duty (conditions precedent), or excuse performance of a duty (conditions subsequent). Failure of a condition will excuse the other party from performing promises made subject to the occurrence of the condition. Failure of a condition might therefore either prevent a duty from becoming absolute, or might excuse the other party from performing its duties. Conditions may be either express or implied.

         Example: Insurer promised to pay for any loss to Farmer's corn crop. The policy required Farmer to preserve any damaged crops pending an inspection by Insurer. After a storm, Farmer plowed the damaged corn stalks before Insurer had a chance to inspect. If the "preservation pending inspection" provision was a condition to the Insurer's duty to pay, the Insurer's duty to pay did not mature. If "preservation" was only a promise, its failure does not excuse the Insurer from paying, but instead, only gives it a right to offset damages it suffered from any payment due to the farmer under the policy.

      3) **Ambiguous Terms Are Construed as Promises Not Conditions.** The parties' intent will control, but any uncertainty or ambiguity in the nature of a term will be construed in favor of treating it as a promise rather than as a condition. This is particularly true where construction of the term as a condition will result in a forfeiture or unjust enrichment. Words such as "subject to" "on condition that", or "provided that" are usually construed as express conditions.

b. **Term Establishing Time for Performance Not a Condition.** A term requiring payment "when" an event occurs is usually construed as specifying the time for performance, not a condition.

Example: General Contractor's promise to pay Sub-Contractor "when" General receives payment from Owner will likely be treated as specifying the time for payment and not as a condition, making General's duty to pay subject to a condition that he first receive payment from the Owner. Treating the term as a condition would result in forfeiture by the Sub-Contractor, depriving him of payment for the value of his work.

2. **Express and Implied Conditions.** Conditions can be expressly stated in the contract or implied from the circumstances surrounding the contract.

a. **Express Conditions** are usually phrased in terms such as "if," "subject to," "on the condition that," "provided that," or similar language removing any doubt about the nature of the term as a condition.

b. **Implied Conditions** arise from the circumstances surrounding the contract indicating that the parties likely intended the imposition of the condition but failed to make it express.

Example: Musician and Theatre agree that Musician will appear at the theatre for a performance on June 15. On June 12, through no fault of either party, the theatre burns to the ground. The continued existence of the theatre will be treated as an **implied condition** of the parties' respective obligations. Its failure excuses both parties from their contractual obligations.

3. **Conditions Are Classified as Precedent, Concurrent, or Subsequent.**

a. **Conditions Precedent**. A condition precedent is a condition that must occur before the promisor's duty matures. If the condition fails to occur, the person whose promise is subject to the condition has no duty to perform. E.g., "If it rains tomorrow, I'll give you a ride" is a promise to provide a ride that does not ripen or become absolute unless it rains.

Example: Insurer promises to pay for loss to Homeowner's furniture, "provided that Homeowner provides notice to Insurer of the loss within 10 days." Notice within 10 days of the loss is a condition precedent to Insurer's duty to pay.

1) **Burden of Proof of Occurrence of Condition Precedent**. When a promise is subject to a condition precedent, the party alleging breach of the promise has the burden of pleading and proof of the occurrence of the condition.

b. **Concurrent Conditions**. Concurrent conditions exist when both parties' performance is subject to conditions precedent that must occur at the same time. Performance of each party's promise is a condition of each party's duty to perform.

Example: Seller promises to sell his car to Buyer in exchange for Buyer's payment of $5,000 cash. Seller's tender of delivery of the car and Buyer's tender of the $5,000 are concurrent conditions. Seller's tender of the car is a condition precedent of Buyer's duty to pay the $5,000; and Buyer's tender of the $5,000 is a condition precedent of Seller's duty to deliver the car.

c. **Condition Subsequent.** The occurrence of a condition subsequent relieves a party from performing a duty, e.g., "I'll take you to the airport tomorrow, unless my sister needs to use the car."

1) **Burden of Proof of Occurrence of Condition Subsequent.** The defendant, who has not performed his promise because of the failure of a condition subsequent, has the burden of proving that the condition excusing performance of his duty has occurred.

4. **Conditions of "Satisfaction" or "Approval."** Conditions of satisfaction make one party's duty to perform subject to the condition of "satisfactory" performance by the other party. This usually occurs when one party promises to pay if he is "satisfied" with the performance rendered by the other, or where the duty to pay depends on the approval of some third party.

a. **Satisfaction or Approval of a Party To the Contract.** Where satisfaction or approval of a party to the contract is a condition of that party's duty to perform, the party must act **reasonably** in exercising judgment about his or her satisfaction or approval. The reasonableness standard is particularly applicable where unjust enrichment will occur if the condition is not met. Some courts require any dissatisfaction to be **reasonable** where failure of the condition would result in either unjust enrichment or forfeiture, such as where a seller will not be paid for specially manufactured goods. The reasonableness standard is also usually applied where artistic or aesthetic judgment is not required. However, absent unjust enrichment, courts adhere to the **subjective good faith** standard where the nature of the performance involves matters of "taste or fancy." Where good faith is the standard, dissatisfaction may not be used as a false pretense to avoid performance.

1) **Condition of Satisfaction Does Not Render the Contract Illusory.** Promises involving unlimited discretion are sometimes unenforceable because of the lack of consideration due to the illusory nature of the discretionary performance. The obligation of good faith or reasonable satisfaction imposes a sufficient restraint on the discretion to prevent the contract from being unenforceable as an illusory promise. Thus, contracts subject to a condition of "satisfactory" performance are enforceable.

Example: Contractor agreed to build swimming pool in Homeowner's back yard, with Homeowner's duty to pay subject to Contractor's "satisfactory" performance. Homeowner's dissatisfaction must be reasonable; otherwise Homeowner would be unjustly enriched.

Example: Artist agreed to paint portrait of Customer's wife, with Customer promising to pay if he was "satisfied" with the portrait. Customer's dissatisfaction will be judged according to a subjective good faith standard even though this may result in a forfeiture of the Artist's effort.

Example: Theatre agreed to pay Musician for "satisfactory" performance by Musician. Theatre claimed "dissatisfaction" and sought to avoid payment when ticket sales were not as expected, though Musician's performance was satisfactory by any reasonable standard. Theatre may not use weak ticket sales as pretense for dissatisfaction with Musician's performance.

b. **Satisfaction of a Third Party**. Where the satisfaction of some third-party is required, that party's satisfaction will be subject to a subjective good faith standard, even where the dissatisfaction is unreasonable. Unreasonableness of dissatisfaction can be used, however, as evidence of subjective bad faith or dishonesty.

Example: Homeowner's duty to pay Contractor for house is subject to condition of satisfaction of Architect. Architect's good faith dissatisfaction with Contractor's performance excuses Homeowner from making final progress payment. Objective compliance with specifications will, however, be used to demonstrate dishonesty, fraud, or lack of good faith of Architect's expression of dissatisfaction.

5. **Constructive Conditions Arising from Bilateral Contracts**. In bilateral contracts, where the parties have exchanged promises, performance of each party's promise can be a "constructive" condition on the other party's duty to perform. Such **constructive conditions** are not express conditions, but are implied from the circumstances of the contract.

a. **Constructive Conditions in Bilateral Contracts.** Where the parties' contract consists of an exchange of promises, with performance of each promise due in the future, the performances are construed as being rendered in exchange for and dependent on one another. Thus, in a contract for the sale of goods, involving a promise of delivery of the goods in exchange for a promise of payment, the duty to deliver the goods is dependent upon payment of the price. Likewise, the duty to pay is dependent upon delivery of the goods. Failure of the seller to deliver the goods excuses the buyer from paying; failure of the buyer to pay excuses the seller from delivering. In this respect, performance of each party's performance is treated constructively as a condition of the other party's duty to provide the return performance.

b. **Concurrent Constructive Conditions – Performances Due Simultaneously.** Where possible, performances are construed as being due simultaneously. Although there is a presumption in favor of simultaneous performance, the parties' intent, as reflected in the circumstances, might indicate that simultaneous performance is not required. Thus, in contracts for the sale of goods and real estate, the duties of the buyer and seller are due simultaneously, unless some aspect of the transaction indicates that simultaneous performance was not intended.

Example: Seller promises to sell automobile in exchange for Buyer's promise to pay. Seller's duty to tender goods is a condition of Buyer's duty to pay and Buyer's duty to pay is a condition of Seller's duty to deliver the goods. If Buyer fails to tender payment at the time and place for performance, Seller's duty to deliver goods does not mature.

Example: Contract for sale of Greenacre between Vendor and Vendee requires Vendor to convey "good title free of any encumbrances" and requires Vendee to tender payment in cash. Greenacre is subject to a mortgage in favor of First Bank. Customarily this type of transaction contemplates that the Vendor will use the price paid by the Vendee to satisfy the mortgage, thus enabling the Vendor to convey good title. In this situation, the vendor has the right to perform at a closing involving all three parties, the Vendor, the Vendee, and the Mortgage holder to facilitate performance of the Vendor's obligation to convey good title.

c. **Performance Not Due Simultaneously.** Circumstances may indicate that the parties' performances are not due simultaneously. This typically occurs in service or construction contracts where one party's performance requires time to complete.

1) **Construction and Employment Contracts**. In construction and employment contracts, performance is usually due before payment. Thus, performance of the promised services is a constructive condition of the recipient's duty to pay.

Example: Resident and Contractor enter into an agreement for construction of an addition to Resident's home. Absent an agreement to the contrary, payment is due upon completion of the Contractor's work. Completion of the addition is a constructive condition of Resident's duty to pay.

2) **Express Terms for Successive Performance.** The parties may expressly agree to any order of performance, such as where, in a construction contract, the recipient agrees to make some sort of partial or even complete payment in advance.

d. **Divisible Contracts.** Contracts are sometimes treated as "divisible" where the parties' performance can be divided into discrete portions. Thus payment for part performance is due even though total performance has not been provided and the "constructive condition" of performance has not occurred. Divisibility is used, where possible, to avoid a forfeiture and unjust enrichment.

Watch Out!

Contracts are divisible only where:

- it is possible to apportion the parties' performances into corresponding parts; and
- each parties' duties to perform an apportioned part can properly be viewed as agreed equivalents for one another.

Example: Shopping Center contracts with Snow Removal Contractor to plow snow from Shopping Center's five like-sized parking lots for a price of $5,000. Contractor only removes snow from two of the five lots. The court might conclude that the contract was divisible into five portions, with the price apportioned equally among each portion. Under these circumstances the Contractor would be entitled to payment of $2,000 for the two lots completed, but would, of course, be liable for damages for breach due to its failure to complete the other three lots.

1) **Apportionment.** Divisibility is permitted only where the contract can be divided into apportioned parts. The price for each part must be susceptible of determination.

   Example: Contractor agrees to excavate land and install foundation for a building to be constructed for a price of $5,000. Absent separate pricing for the excavation and installation, there is no way to apportion the price between the two performances due.

2) **Equivalent Exchanges.** Even if the contract can be apportioned, the court will treat the contract as divisible only if each party's apportioned performance can be viewed as an equivalent exchange.

   Example: Seller agrees to sell three contiguous parcels of real estate to Buyer for $300,000 where it is contemplated that Buyer will build an office building covering all three parcels. The Seller is able to convey good title to only 2 of the 3 parcels. Though the price might be apportioned, $100,000 for each parcel, the circumstances indicate that the price for the 3 parcels together was greater than the value of each lot individually because conveyance of only two parcels would not permit construction of the office building.

3) **Installment Contracts for the Sale of Goods.** In contracts for the sale of goods under circumstances which provide for or permit the seller to deliver the goods in more than one installment, unless otherwise agreed the seller has the right, under UCC 2-307, to insist on proportional payment for each installment delivery as it is made.

Example: Buyer and Seller enter into an agreement for delivery of 10 truckloads of bricks. Seller may insist on payment for each truckload as it is delivered, and Buyer may not refuse to wait until all 10 truckloads before making any payment.

6. **Independent Promises.** Promises are sometimes intended to be independent of one another. A promise is treated as independent and unconditional if it does not depend on performance of the other party's promises.

B. EXCUSE OF CONDITIONS

Conditions may be excused due to waiver, estoppel, interference, impossibility or frustration of purpose, repudiation, or breach. Constructive conditions, implied from promises, may be substantially performed.

1. **Effect of Excuse of Condition**. If a condition is excused, the party whose performance depends on occurrence of the condition may not assert the failure of the condition to avoid performing his or her duties under the contract.

2. **Excuse Due To Interference, Breach, or Repudiation**.

   a. **Interference.** Each party has a duty of good faith that prevents engaging in conduct which would interfere with or prevent the occurrence of a condition to his own performance. A party whose own conduct interferes with or prevents the occurrence of a condition, whether or not it also amounts to a breach or repudiation, cannot assert the resulting failure of the condition to avoid liability for breach. A party may be required to take affirmative reasonable steps to ensure the occurrence of a condition.

   Example: Buyer agrees to purchase Greenacre, subject to the condition of the availability of a mortgage loan. Buyer fails to apply for loan and then attempts to use the failure of the condition as a basis for refusing to purchase the land. Buyer's failure to take the reasonable step of applying for the loan prevents Buyer from asserting the condition as a justification for refusing to perform.

   Example: Seller agrees to deliver goods to Buyer as selected by Buyer. Seller fails to provide samples to Buyer from which to make his selection. Seller cannot assert the Buyer's failure to make the necessary selection as a justification for refusing to deliver the goods.

   b. **Breach.** Breach by one party that causes a condition not to occur excuses the condition. Thus, a party may not use the effects of his own breach as a justification for not performing.

   c. **Repudiation.** Likewise, where a party's repudiation of his obligations under the contract causes a condition to fail to occur, the party may not use his own repudiation of the contract to avoid his own obligations.

3. **Excuse Due To Waiver or Estoppel.** Conditions may be expressly or impliedly waived. Likewise, a party may be estopped from asserting the failure of a condition if he induced the other party to believe that the condition would not be asserted.

   a. **Waiver.** Waiver is the **intentional relinquishment of a known right** and may be express or implied. An express waiver occurs when a party promises to perform a conditional duty even if the condition is not performed. An implied waiver is similar to estoppel, and is implied from conduct indicating that performance will occur despite the failure of a condition.

      1) **Waiver as Unenforceable Modification.** An attempt to expressly waive a condition before the time for occurrence of the condition has passed may be treated as an attempt to modify the contract without consideration. Where the other party reasonably relies on the expressed waiver, however, the condition will be excused due to **promissory estoppel.** A party cannot reassert a condition after inducing the other to detrimentally rely on waiver of the condition. If consideration is not necessary for modification, the waiver may be an enforceable modification of the contract. For example, consideration is no longer necessary, as specified by UCC 2-209, for a good faith modification of a contract for the sale of goods.

         Example: Construction contract requires Contractor to supply a certificate from Architect before receipt of progress payments from Owner. Owner promises Contractor that he will make payments without the need to provide an architect's certificate. This promise is an attempt to modify the contract and will not be enforceable, due to the lack of consideration, as a modification of the contract. However, where the Contractor relies on the promise by failing to seek an architect's certificate, such as by continuing with construction in a way that makes the architect's inspection impossible, the waiver will be effective.

      2) **Waiver of Material Condition Ineffective.** An express waiver of a condition that is a material part of the bargain is usually not effective. Thus, a Homeowner who enters into a contract to pay his nephew $1,000 in exchange for Nephew's agreement to mow Homeowner's lawn for the entire summer cannot effectively waive the constructive condition that Nephew mow the lawn.

      3) **Retraction of Waiver**. A waiver may be retracted, with respect to an uncompleted or "executory" portion of the contract, at any time upon **reasonable notice.** Detrimental reliance on the waiver may prevent retraction.

   b. **Estoppel.** A party who performs a conditional duty, despite the non-occurrence of the condition, may be estopped from asserting the failure of the condition with respect to future performances. Estoppel usually arises in the context of successive performances, over a period of time, where one party performs despite the failure of the other party to strictly perform an express or constructive condition of those duties. Thus, a buyer who pays for goods even though they are delivered late may be estopped from asserting timely delivery as a condition of its duty to pay in the future. Likewise, a landlord, who accepts rent paid late, may be estopped from seeking to evict a tenant who fails to make subsequent payments on time.

4. **Election**. An election is a choice by a party not to assert the failure of the condition after the time for occurrence of a condition has passed. A party who elects to ignore the failure of a condition cannot subsequently assert the condition to avoid performance.

   Example: Insurance contract conditions Insurer's duty on formal written notice of casualty. Insurer makes preliminary payment for partial loss after deadline for formal notice. The insurer has elected not to assert the condition and will be prevented from asserting its failure even though the Insured has not relied to its detriment in any way on the election.

5. **Impossibility or Frustration of Purpose**. An **ancillary condition** may be excused due to impossibility or frustration of purpose where assertion of the condition would result in forfeiture. The impossibility must be due **to circumstances beyond the control** of the party who has the obligation to perform the condition. The condition must be ancillary to the contract and not a material part of the obligee's duties under the agreement. Impossibility of this type frequently arises in the context of insurance contracts where the insured is unable to perform a condition requiring timely notice due to the consequences of the very casualty that gave rise to the claim.

   Example: Auto Insurance Policy requires notice within 10 days of the occurrence of an insured casualty loss. The Insured was rendered unconscious in an auto accident and did not regain consciousness until two weeks after the wreck. The condition of notice within 10 days is at least suspended until the Insured regains her capacity to provide the necessary notice.

   Example: Insurance Policy is conditional on timely payment of premiums. Failure of the Insured to make timely payments, due to the intervention of war, is not excused.

6. **Excuse Due To Disproportionate Forfeiture and Unjust Enrichment**. Where one party would receive a substantial benefit at the expense of the other if the condition is not excused, the court will excuse the condition to the extent necessary to prevent the forfeiture. This can occur when a construction contract makes the use of certain brands of materials a condition of the Owner's duty to pay even though the value of the completed construction is the same regardless of what brand is used.

   Example: Owner of goods contracts with Carrier for the transportation of the goods from New York to San Francisco, and promises to pay for their transport on condition that the goods are transported "by rail." The goods are transported by truck and delivered on time. Owner will be unjustly enriched and Carrier will suffer forfeiture unless condition of transportation by rail is excused.

7. **Substantial Performance of Constructive Condition.** In cases involving constructive conditions, implied from bilateral promises, substantial performance of a promise, which fulfills the basic purpose of the contract, satisfies the constructive condition on the other party's duty to perform. It is sometimes said that "substantial performance" excuses performance of a constructive condition. It is more accurate to say that "substantial performance" *is* the constructive condition and that promises must be substantially performed for the other party's duties to mature.

8. **Aleatory Promises.** An aleatory promise is one that is subject to the occurrence of some uncertain or fortuitous event. Insurance contracts are examples of aleatory promises. The insurer's duty to pay is subject to the occurrence of some condition or event, usually a casualty to the insured property or person. In cases involving aleatory promises, the promisor's duty depends entirely upon the occurrence of the condition. Occurrence of the principal conditions, upon which the promise depends, cannot be waived or excused. Other minor conditions, such as giving notice of the casualty, may be excused where waived.

C. BREACH AND ITS CONSEQUENCES

Breach of contract occurs where there is an unexcused failure to render a matured duty in accordance with the terms of the contract. The consequences of a breach depend on whether it is a material or minor breach and, if material, if it is a total material breach or merely a partial material breach.

1. **Material Breach and Substantial Performance.** A material breach is one that deprives the innocent party of the substantial benefit of the bargain. Substantial performance is performance that, though not complete, fulfills the essential purpose of the contract. Substantial performance does not constitute material breach and a material breach does not qualify as substantial performance. In this respect, material breach and substantial performance are two sides of the same coin.

2. **Distinguishing Material Breach from Minor Breach.** Whether a particular breach is material depends upon the nature of the contract and the circumstances surrounding the breach. Where the breach is minor, there has been **substantial performance.** A variety of factors are used by Restatement 2d §§ 241-242 in determining whether a breach is material, including:

    a. the extent of the innocent party's **loss of the substantial benefits** reasonably expected under the contract;

    b. the **adequacy of money damages** to compensate for the breach;

    c. the **extent of the forfeiture** suffered by the breaching party as a result of the breach if the breach is treated as material;

    d. **the likelihood of cure** by the breaching party; and

e. whether the breach was **willful, negligent, inadvertent, or in good faith**.

Example: Contractor agreed to build office building for Owner, with construction to be completed by June 15th to permit tenants to move in no later than July 1st. Contractor did not complete performance until June 17th, which still left time for tenants to move in by July 1st. Delayed completion did not deprive the Owner of any substantial benefits under the contract and treating the breach as material would result in an extreme forfeiture by the Contractor. The Contractor has substantially performed. Owner can recover any damages it can prove as a consequence of the minor delay.

Example: Same facts as above, but due to negligent performance, Contractor did not complete construction until August 15. Delay has substantially impaired value of timely completion to Owner by preventing Owner from fulfilling obligations to its tenants or from collecting rent from tenants who had contracts entitling them to move in on July 1. This is a material breach that will justify Owner in suspending performance due to the breach.

3. **Effect of Material Breach.** Material breach permits the non-breaching party to pursue any right to money damages or equitable remedies for breach and to **suspend performance** of its duties under the contract.

    a. **A Material Breach May Be Total or Partial Breach**.

    b. **Partial Breach.** Where there has been a partial material breach the non-breaching party may:

        1) **suspend performance** of its own duties under the contract;

        2) provide the breaching party with an **opportunity to cure**; and

        3) **recover damages** for any loss suffered as a result of the breach.

    c. **Partial Breach May Become Total.** A partial breach may become a total breach if the breaching party does not provide a timely cure for the breach.

    d. **Total Breach.** When the breach is total, the aggrieved party may:

        1) **terminate (or rescind) the contract;**

        2) **cease performance** of its own duties; and

        3) **recover damages** for any loss suffered as a result of the breach.

Example: Bridge Builder entered into contract with Sub-Contractor to have Sub-Contractor coat Bridge Builder's two main bridge components with anti-corrosive material to prevent rust. Sub-Contractor misapplied the anti-corrosive material to the first bridge component which resulted in the ineffectiveness of the anti-corrosive material. Bridge Builder suspended payments due under the contract, refusing to pay until Sub-Contractor corrected the defect. In response, Sub-Contractor refused to continue work. Because misapplication of the anti-corrosive material substantially impaired the value of the contract, the misapplication was a partial material breach and Bridge Builder was justified in suspending its own performance while waiting for Sub-Contractor to cure. Because Bridge Builder was justified in suspending its performance, Sub-Contractor's refusal to continue its work was a total material breach that would justify Bridge Builder in terminating its performance under the contract. Sub-Contractor's partial material breach became a total material breach when Sub-Contractor refused to continue performing.

4. **Effect of Minor Breach.** A minor or non-material breach permits the non-breaching party to recover damages for breach. However, a minor breach does not relieve the non-breaching party from its obligation to continue to perform its obligations under the contract. This is the principal distinction between a material and non-material or minor breach.

5. **Cure.** A breaching party may sometimes cure a breach even though it is material. Cure may consist of repairing any defective performance, correcting defects in title, or making payment, though late, with any interest necessary to compensate for the delay.

   a. **Seller's Right To Cure in Contract for Sale of Goods under UCC 2-508.** In contracts for the sale of goods, the seller has a right to cure in two situations: 1) where defective goods are delivered before time for performance has expired; 2) and, even where the time for performance has expired, if the seller had reason to believe that the goods would be acceptable to the buyer. The seller must give timely notice of its intent to cure. Cure will usually consist of repair or replacement of the defective goods.

   Example: Seller contracted to deliver a Model 2000 bicycle frame to Buyer for price of $1700. At time for performance Seller delivered updated 2001 Model bicycle frame. After inspection, Buyer rejected Model 2001 because it was not the 2000 model and he did not like the updated features of the 2001 Seller delivered. Because the goods did not conform to the specifications of the contract, Buyer is justified in rejecting the updated 2001 model. Because Seller had reason to believe 2001 model would be acceptable to Buyer, Seller has a right to cure by delivering the 2000 model specified in the contract, even though time for performance has expired.

6. **Anticipatory Repudiation.**
   Anticipatory repudiation, sometimes called anticipatory breach, occurs when a party unequivocally communicates its intent not to perform the contract or when a party insists upon conditions that go beyond the contract. Communication of an intent not to perform may be by **language or conduct**, so long as it unequivocally indicates that performance will not occur.

   a. **Effect of Anticipatory Repudiation**. Repudiation, before the breaching party has substantially performed, permits the aggrieved party to treat the repudiation as a total breach and:

      1) **suspend or terminate its own performance;**

      2) **ignore the repudiation and wait for a commercially reasonable time** for the repudiating party to retract its repudiation or resume performance. Once a reasonable time has passed, however, the aggrieved party must treat the contract as terminated and cease its own performance; and

      3) **recover damages** for any losses caused by the breach.

   b. **Repudiation after Substantial Performance.** Repudiation by a party after it has substantially performed may not be treated as a total breach. The aggrieved party may await full performance or sue to recover damages caused by the failure to fully perform.

   c. **Retraction of Repudiation.** A party who has repudiated may retract its repudiation and resume performance so long as the innocent party has not materially changed its position as a result of the repudiation.

      Example: Employer fires Employee, without cause, in breach of a three year employment contract. Employee immediately seeks and obtains employment elsewhere. Employer then retracts repudiation and implores Employee to return. Employer's retraction came too late, after Employee had materially changed his position by entering into a contract of employment with someone else.

   d. **Anticipatory Repudiation in Contracts for Sale of Goods.** In Contracts for the sale of goods under UCC 2-610, when either the Buyer or the Seller repudiates with respect to a delivery not yet due, and loss of the performance would substantially impair the value of the contract to the non-breaching party, the non-breaching party may wait for a commercially reasonable time, suspend its own performance, and resort to any remedy provided for breach, even if he has urged retraction and notified the repudiating party that he will wait for performance.

7. **Prospective Inability to Perform.** Reasonable grounds to doubt the ability of the other party to perform does not permit the doubting party to suspend or terminate its own performance. But a party may be permitted to demand adequate assurance of performance.

8. **Right to Adequate Assurance of Performance in Contracts for the Sale of Goods.** UCC 2-609 alters the traditional rule and gives a party the right to demand adequate assurances of future performance whenever there are "reasonable grounds for insecurity" with respect to a future performance.

   a. **Reasonable Grounds for Insecurity.** Grounds must be based on information from a reliable source and not mere rumors of financial difficulty or other circumstances that would make performance difficult or impossible.

   b. **Demand for Adequate Assurance of Performance.** Demand must be made in writing.

   c. **Suspension of Performance.** Party seeking assurance may, while awaiting assurance, **suspend performance of its own duties** for which it has not already received the agreed return, if it is commercially reasonable to do so.

      Example: Contract for sale of goods requires Seller to deliver goods before payment. Before time for delivery, Seller learns, from another of Buyer's suppliers, that Buyer is insolvent and has suspended payments for goods already delivered by the other supplier. Based on this solid information from a reliable source, Seller is justified in making a written demand for adequate assurance of payment for goods yet to be delivered and in suspending delivery pending receipt of adequate assurances. Seller may not, however, refuse to deliver goods for which payment has already been made.

   d. **Adequate Assurances of Performance Due Within Reasonable Time Not More Than 30 Days.** When a warranted demand for assurances has been made, **adequate assurance** must be provided within a reasonable time, but not more than 30 days.

   e. **Failure To Provide Adequate Assurance Treated as Repudiation**. Any failure to provide adequate assurance of performance is a repudiation. The repudiation is treated as any other, permitting the aggrieved party to terminate its own performance, to seek damages for breach or resort to any other remedy, or, to ignore the failure to provide assurances and await performance for a commercially reasonable time.

9. **Other Contracts: Right to Adequate Assurance of Performance.** The traditional rule does not give the uncertain party grounds to demand assurances of performance, except in the limited circumstances where the other party was insolvent. Modern courts have altered the traditional rule and have applied UCC 2-609 by analogy to transactions other than those involving a sale of goods to permit a party with reasonable grounds for insecurity to demand adequate assurance of performance. The Restatement (2d) of

Contracts has adopted the doctrine of adequate assurances in § 251, but not all jurisdictions have embraced § 251.

D. WARRANTIES

1. **Express Warranties in Contracts for Sale of Goods.** Under UCC 2-313, an express warranty is made by the seller by any **1) affirmation of fact or promise which relates to the goods; 2) any description of the goods; or 3) any sample or model** which is made a **part of the basis of the bargain**.

    a. **Reliance Not Required; "Basis of the Bargain."** Reliance by the buyer is not necessary for the creation of an express warranty. It is sufficient if the affirmation of fact, promise, description, sample or model is **part of the basis of the bargain.** The part of the basis of the bargain test is always satisfied when the buyer knew or had reason to know of the warranty at the time the contract for sale was made.

    b. **Express Warranty in Absence of Words "Warranty" or "Guaranty."** A warranty will exist even if the seller does not use terms such as "warranty" or "guaranty," or even if the seller does not have the subjective intent to provide a warranty, so long as there is an affirmation of fact, promise, description, sample, or model used in connection with the sale.

    c. **Mere Opinion Is Not an Express Warranty.** A mere expression of **opinion**, commendation or affirmation of the value of the goods does not provide an express warranty. Mere "puffing" that does not amount to an affirmation of fact, promise, or description, does not give rise to a warranty.

2. **Implied Warranties**

    a. **Implied Warranty of Merchantability**. Under UCC 2-314, every contract for **sale of goods by a merchant** contains an implied warranty that the goods will be **of merchantable quality**. The implied warranty can apply to used as well as new goods. Implied warranties may be disclaimed.

        1) **Goods Must Be Fit For Their Ordinary Purpose.** The basic test for merchantability is that the goods must be **fit for the ordinary purpose** of the goods involved.

        Example: Buyer purchases an automobile from Auto Dealer. Shortly after purchase, the steering wheel of the auto veers out of control making it impossible for Buyer to steer the car. Because the seller was an Auto Dealer who deals in goods of the kind, there is a warranty of merchantability. The inability to steer the car makes it unsuitable for the ordinary purpose of driving on roads and the warranty of merchantability has been breached.

2) **To Be Merchantable Goods Must Also:**

   a) pass without objection in the trade under the description;

   b) in the case of fungible goods, be of fair average quality within the description;

   c) run, within the variations permitted by the agreement, of even kind, quality, and quantity within and among units;

   d) be adequately contained, packaged, and labeled; and

   e) conform to any promise or affirmations of fact made on any container or label.

   Example: Restaurant serves wine to Customer in glass, which shatters, injuring Customer's hand. Wine was not merchantable because it was contained in an inadequate glass.

3) **Possibility of Disclaimer.** The implied warranty of merchantability can be effectively disclaimed under UCC 2-316 through a conspicuous disclaimer that uses the term **merchantability**.

b. **Implied Warranty of Fitness for Particular Purpose.** There is an implied warranty that the goods will be fit for their particular purpose where **at the time the contract is made** the **seller has reason to know of the buyer's particular purpose** and has reason to know that the **buyer is relying on the seller's skill or judgment** in selecting or furnishing the goods.

   1) The warranty of particular purpose can be disclaimed via written and conspicuous language indicating that the seller is not making any warranties beyond the face of the writing.

   2) The seller does **not** have to be a merchant for the implied warranty of fitness for particular purpose to apply.

c. **Implied Warranty of Title under UCC 2-312.** Every contract for the sale of goods contains a warranty of good title. The warranty is that the buyer will have **good title**, that **the transfer to the buyer is rightful**, and that the seller has **no knowledge of any security interest** or lien that will encumber the goods in the hands of the buyer.

   1) The fact that the seller's title is encumbered by a security interest, in favor of the seller's lender, will not result in a breach of the warranty of good title where the buyer is a buyer in the ordinary course of business who obtains the goods free of any such security interest under UCC 9-307(1).

2) The warranty of good title can be effectively disclaimed, but only by specific knowledge or circumstances which give the buyer reason to know that the seller does not claim good title in himself.

3) A seller who is a merchant regularly dealing in goods of the kind also makes a warranty that the goods will be delivered free of any rightful claim of patent, trademark or other infringement. However, a buyer who supplies specifications to the seller for the goods must hold the seller harmless against any claim of infringement which arises out of the seller's compliance with those specifications.

d. **Real Estate -- Implied Warranty of Habitability.** In contracts for the sale of a new home, courts have implied a warranty that the structure will be fit for habitability analogous to the UCC's implied warranty that goods will be merchantable.

3. **Disclaimers of Warranties under UCC 2-316**

a. **Disclaimer of Express Warranties**. Any attempt to disclaim express warranties will be construed, where possible, as consistent with any express warranty, but where the terms of an express warranty and a disclaimer conflict, the warranty will prevail.

1) The claim of warranty must be consistent with the provisions of the parol evidence rule of UCC 2-202.

b. **Disclaimer of Implied Warranty of Merchantability**. Any disclaimer of the implied warranty of merchantability must be **conspicuous** and must use the word **merchantability.**

c. **Disclaimer of Warranty of Fitness for Particular Purpose.** A disclaimer of the warranty of fitness for particular purpose must be in writing and conspicuous. Language indicating that "there are no warranties which extend beyond the description of the face hereof" is sufficient, but other similar language is permitted.

d. **Alternate Methods of Disclaiming Warranties**

1) **Other Language.** Implied warranties of merchantability and fitness can also be disclaimed by conspicuous use of terms such as **"as is"** or **"with all faults"** or other language, which in common understanding calls attention to the absence of a warranty and makes plain that there is no implied warranty.

2) **Buyer's Inspection or Opportunity To Inspect.** There is no implied warranty with respect to defects an inspection ought to have revealed where: a) the buyer has examined the goods before entering into a contract; b) the buyer has examined a sample or model as fully as desired; or c) the buyer has refused to examine the goods.

3) **Course of Dealing, Usage of Trade, or Course of Performance**. Implied warranties can also be excluded by a course of dealing, usage of trade, or course of performance.

4. **Defenses To Warranties**. Even when a warranty has not been effectively disclaimed, the seller may have a defense based on **lack of privity, contributory negligence or assumption of the risk, the statute of limitations, or failure to give timely notice of breach of the warranty.**

   a. **Lack of Privity.** An action for breach of warranty could traditionally only be made by someone who was in "privity of contract" with the breaching party. Persons who were not parties to the contract lacked privity. Parties lacking privity can be divided into two categories: vertical non-privity and horizontal non-privity. In contracts for the sale of goods, UCC 2-318 replaces the common law limitations on both vertical and horizontal non-privity and permits some persons who were not a party to the original contract to recover for breach of the seller's warranty despite their lack of privity.

      1) **Vertical Privity.** Vertical privity refers to the relationship between parties in the chain of distribution of goods such as from manufacturer to distributor to retailer to consumer. Thus a distributor who buys goods from a manufacturer is in privity with the manufacturer because they were parties to the same contract of sale. The distributor could recover from the manufacturer for damages caused to the distributor by any breach of the manufacturer's warranties. However, a retailer or consumer, who purchased the goods from the distributor, was not a party to the contract between the manufacturer and the distributor and therefore lacked vertical privity with the manufacturer and could not recover for any breach of the manufacturer's warranty regarding the goods.

      2) **Horizontal Privity.** Horizontal privity refers to the relationship between the buyer of the goods, and others who either consume the goods or are affected by them. Horizontal privity problems usually arise when those associated with the end user or consumer are harmed by the goods, such as when a member of the buyer's family or a guest in the buyer's house is harmed by the goods. The family member or guest is not in privity with the seller and thus could not recover for breach of the seller's warranty to the buyer.

      3) **Alternative Privity Rules in UCC 2-318**. UCC 2-318 contains three alternative privity rules that extend a seller's **express or implied warranties** to those not in vertical or horizontal privity with the seller. Sellers **may not** exclude or limit the effect of these provisions to the extent that they impose liability for **personal injury.**

         a) **Alternative A.** Alternative A extends a seller's express or implied warranties to any **natural person** who is in the **family or household of the buyer, or a guest in the buyer's home** if it is **reasonable to expect that person to use or**

consume goods or be affected by the goods and who suffers **personal injury** from the goods as a result of the breach of warranty.

b) **Alternative B.** Alternative B extends the seller's express or implied warranties further to **any natural person who may reasonably be expected to use, consume or be affected** by the goods and who suffers **personal injury.**

Example: A Restaurant purchases tainted eggs from a Distributor and serves them to its Customers who become ill due to salmonella poisoning. The Customers could recover from the Distributor, under alternative B, despite their lack of privity, but not under Alternative A because they were not members of the Restaurant's family or guests in the home of the Buyer.

c) **Alternative C**. Alternative C extends the seller's express or implied warranties to **any person** who may reasonably be expected to use, consume, or be affected by the goods and **who is injured** by the breach of warranty. The protection of Alternative C extends beyond natural persons to protect corporations, partnerships and others. Further, it provides protection for loss due to **property damage and direct economic loss** to persons who lack privity with the seller. The only limit on warranty protection imposed by Alternative C is that the person harmed by the breach of warranty must **reasonably be expected to use, consume, or be affected** by the goods.

d) **Strict Product Liability in Tort**. Where personal injury is involved, liability may extend beyond that provided by any of the alternative versions of UCC 2-318 by Restatement of Torts § 402A and Strict Product Liability in Tort for Unreasonably Defective Products.

b. **Plaintiff's Contributory Negligence or Misuse.** Contributory negligence of the plaintiff in negligently handling the goods or misusing the goods can sometimes be used as a defense to a breach of warranty action. Courts sometimes say that contributory negligence is not a defense, but nevertheless permit the plaintiff's conduct to be used to limit or eliminate the seller's liability by characterizing the issue as a break in the chain of **proximate cause** of the plaintiff's injuries.

c. **Four-Year Statute of Limitations.** The statute of limitations in actions for breach of a contract for the sale of goods, including breach of warranty, under UCC 2-725, is **four years from the time the cause of action has accrued.**

1) **Accrual of Cause of Action.** The accrual of a cause of action is usually when **tender of delivery** is made. This is true despite the buyer's failure to discover the defect and despite its difficulty of discovery. Where the defect is particularly difficult to discover, courts have sometimes ruled that the cause of action accrues when the plaintiff discovered or should have discovered the harm.

Example: Defective drug causes harm only after repeated use over a six month period. Cause of action accrues when plaintiff first experienced the drug's harmful effect.

2) **Warranty Explicitly Extends to Future Performance.** Where an express warranty explicitly promises **future performance,** the cause of action does not accrue, under UCC 2-725(2), until the buyer discovers or should have discovered the breach.

   Example: Seller warrants goods for 5 years (or 60 months) from date of purchase. Defect in goods first became manifest 50 months after purchase and tender of delivery. The warranty explicitly extended to future performance of the goods, so the cause of action did not accrue and the statute of limitations did not begin to run until the defect manifested itself, at which time the buyer should have discovered the defect.

3) **Two-Year Statute of Limitations for Strict Product Liability.** Actions based on strict product liability, however, are subject to the standard 2-year tort statute of limitations which begins to run when the defect **causes an injury** or **should have been discovered.**

d. **Buyer's Failure To Give Notice.** UCC 2-607(3)(a) requires a buyer to **notify the seller of breach** within a **reasonable time** after the buyer discovered or should have discovered any breach **or be barred from any remedy.** Thus a buyer who fails to notify the seller of a defect within a reasonable time after it was or should have been discovered will be prevented from obtaining a remedy of either cure, money damages, or revocation of acceptance.

   1) **Form and Contents of the Notice.** To be effective, the notice must be sufficient to let the seller know that there is some trouble still associated with the transaction. The notice need not be in writing, nor must it be provided by any formal mechanism.

5. **Limited Remedies under UCC 2-719**. In addition to disclaiming warranties, remedies for breach of warranty may be limited, such as by a provision limiting remedies to repair or replacement. Though the code does not specify this, limited remedy provisions must be conspicuous. Any attempt to exclude liability for personal injury in the case of consumer goods is prima facie unconscionable, but exclusion of other commercial consequential damages is permitted.

E. PERFORMANCE OF CONTRACTS FOR SALE OF GOODS

Tender, Acceptance, Rejection, Revocation of Acceptance, and Cure

1. **Seller's Duty To Tender Goods.** The seller has a duty to tender goods that conform to the terms of the contract. Under UCC 2-507, the buyer's duty to accept and pay for the goods is subject to an implied concurrent condition of proper tender by the seller.

a. **Tender of Delivery**. Tender occurs when the seller **puts and holds conforming goods** at the buyer's disposition and gives the buyer any **notification reasonably necessary** to enable the buyer to take delivery.

b. **Time for Tender.** The time for tender is determined by the agreement, but must be at a **reasonable hour** and the goods must be kept available for a time reasonably necessary to enable the buyer to take possession.

c. **Place for Tender.** The place for tender is determined by the agreement.

1) **Seller in Possession of Goods**. Where the seller is in possession of the goods and there is no agreement on the place for delivery, the place for delivery under UCC 2-308 is the seller's place of business, or, if the seller has no place of business, then the seller's residence; or if the contract is for sale of identified goods known at the time the contract was made to be in some other place, that place is the place for their delivery.

2) **Bailee in Possession – Delivery Without Transport**. Goods in possession of a bailee to be delivered without being moved. Sometimes, the goods are stored in a warehouse owned by a 3rd party bailee with the intent that they will be delivered to the buyer without being moved out of the warehouse. Tender of delivery is accomplished in these cases via either the sender's delivery of a **document of title**, such as a warehouse receipt or delivery order covering the goods, or the seller obtaining the bailee's acknowledgment of the buyer's right to possession of the goods.

3) **Delivery or Shipment via Carrier**. When the contract requires or permits the seller to ship the goods, proper tender depends on whether the contract is one for "delivery" or "shipment" as explained in the next section.

d. **Delivery or Shipment via Carrier.** In many cases, the contract will require or authorize the seller to send the goods to the buyer via a common carrier such as a trucking company, railroad, airline, etc. Such contracts are usually either "shipment" or "destination" contracts. The "F.O.B." term usually indicates whether it is a shipment or destination contract by designating the place of shipment or the destination.

1) **Destination Contracts**. A "destination" contract requires the seller to deliver the goods at a particular destination. This type of contract contains the mercantile term "F.O.B." designating the destination of the goods.

a) **Seller's Duties Include:**

i) tender of the goods to the buyer at the designated destination at a reasonable hour;

ii) giving the buyer reasonable notification of their tender; and

iii) tender of the documents covering the goods (bill of lading) necessary to obtain them from the carrier. Tender of documents may be made through banking channels.

b) Buyer's Duties Are:

i) to furnish facilities reasonably suited to the receipt of the goods; and

ii) to tender payment upon tender of the documents by the seller.

c) In a destination contract, under UCC 2-508, the risk of casualty loss during transit is on the seller.

Example: Contract provides "F.O.B. Buyer's factory, Memphis." Seller makes a contract for transport of the goods from its factory in Sacramento, to the Buyer's factory in Memphis and delivers the goods to a suitable trucking company. En route to Memphis, the truck is destroyed in a tornado. Because this is a destination contract, the risk of loss is on the seller who has failed to make a proper tender of the goods at the buyer's factory in Memphis.

d) Mercantile terms customarily used in connection with a destination contract are:

i) **"F.O.B. Place of Destination";**

ii) **"F.A.S."** naming a particular ship to which the goods must be delivered for transportation;

iii) "**Ex Ship**" naming the ship from which the goods must be safely unloaded from the ship's tackle at a named destination.

Example: A contract for the sale of widgets provides for a price of "$7,000, F.O.B. Buyer's loading dock". Seller is required to make a contract for the delivery of the goods to Buyer's loading dock and pay for shipment. If the goods are lost during transit, Seller bears the risk of loss.

2) **Shipment Contracts**. A shipment contract is one that **does not** require the seller to deliver the goods at a particular place or destination. Use of an "F.O.B." term designating the place of shipment is a "shipment" contract. In a shipment contract, the seller is not responsible for arrival of the goods at the destination, but only for placing them in the hands of a reasonable carrier and making a reasonable contract for their shipment to the buyer. The seller must also **notify** the buyer of their shipment and tender to the buyer the documents (bill of lading) necessary to obtain them from the carrier.

a) **Presumption of Shipment Contract**. Where the contract requires or authorizes the seller to ship the goods, but does not designate a point of shipment or a destination, the contract is presumed to be a shipment contract.

b) **Seller's Duties in Shipment Contract**. In a shipment contract, the seller has the duty to:

i) put the goods in the possession of a reasonable carrier;

ii) make a reasonable contract for transportation of the goods;

iii) obtain and tender the documents necessary to enable the buyer to obtain possession of the goods; and

iv) promptly notify the buyer of the shipment of the goods; but failure to notify justifies the buyer's rejection only if it causes material delay or loss to the buyer.

c) **Risk of Loss.** In a shipment contract, the risk of casualty loss during transit is on the buyer.

Example: Contract provides "F.O.B. Seller's loading dock, Chicago." Seller makes a contract for transport of the goods from its factory in Chicago, to Buyer's location in Philadelphia and delivers the goods to a suitable trucking company. En route to Philadelphia, the truck carrying the goods is destroyed in a wreck. Seller made a proper tender when the goods were delivered to the trucking company at Seller's Loading Dock, in Chicago. The risk of loss during transit was on Buyer who has a duty to pay for the goods.

3) **Mercantile Terms.**

a) **F.O.B.** means "Free On Board" and is used, **together with a named location**, to indicate a shipment or destination contract.

Example: Contract provides for a price stated as "$10,000, F.O.B. Sellersville" where Sellersville is the location of the seller's place of business. This is a "shipment" contract requiring the seller to deliver the goods to a reasonable carrier and make a reasonable contract for their carriage to the buyer's place of business, with the buyer to pay for the cost of carriage and to incur the risk of loss during transit. The seller is also required to make arrangements for transmittal to the buyer of any documents necessary to obtain the goods from the carrier.

b) **C.I.F. and "C. and F."** referring respectively to "Cost, Insurance, and Freight" and "Cost and Freight" indicate that the buyer is expected to pay for not just the cost of the goods, but also freight, and, where indicated, insurance.

These contracts are always "shipment" contracts even if a buyer's location or some other destination is specified. C.I.F. and C. and F., like C.O.D., indicate that payment is to be made when documents of title, such as a bill of lading, is presented. In such cases the buyer has no right to inspect the goods before payment.

c) **C.O.D.** means "Cash On Delivery" and indicates that the buyer must make payment against documents with no right to inspect the goods prior to payment.

d) **"F.A.S."** means "Free Alongside" and designates a ship or vessel. The term requires the seller to deliver the goods safely shipside for transport to the buyer.

e) **"Ex Ship"** also designates a particular vessel and requires the seller to have the goods delivered safely from the ship's tackle at the designated port of destination.

2. **Buyer's Right of Inspection before Acceptance and Payment** – Unless agreed otherwise, the buyer has a right under UCC 2-513 to inspect the goods before payment or acceptance at any reasonable place, time, and manner.

   a. **Expenses of Inspection.** The expense of inspection is borne by the buyer, but may be shifted to the seller as incidental damages where the goods do not conform.

   b. **No Right To Inspection in Documentary Sales and C.O.D. Contracts.** The buyer has no right to inspection prior to acceptance and payment when the contract provides for payment against a bill of lading, a warehouse receipt or other documents of title, or where the contract is "C.O.D" (cash on delivery).

3. **Acceptance by Buyer**. The buyer's duties include acceptance of conforming goods. Acceptance by the buyer occurs if the buyer signifies acceptance, does any act inconsistent with the seller's ownership, or otherwise fails to make a proper rejection.

   a. **Acceptance by Buyer Signification of Acceptance.** The buyer accepts if, after he has had a chance to inspect the goods, he communicates or otherwise signifies that the goods are conforming or that he will keep them despite any nonconformity.

   b. **Acceptance by Conduct Inconsistent with Seller's Ownership.** The buyer also accepts if he does anything that is incompatible with the seller's ownership of the goods, such as using them other than as part of an inspection in his manufacturing process, reselling them, or otherwise.

   c. **Failure to Properly Reject**. The buyer also accepts if, after any applicable opportunity to inspect the goods, the buyer fails to make a proper rejection within a reasonable time after delivery or tender.

4. **Buyer's Duty To Pay for Accepted Goods.** The buyer has a duty to pay for any goods accepted under the contract. Absent any agreement otherwise, the buyer's duty to pay is a condition to the seller's duty to tender and complete delivery of the goods. Thus, failure of the buyer to make a proper tender of payment excuses the seller from its duty to tender delivery of the goods.

   a. **Time and Place for Payment**. Under UCC 2-310, payment is due at the time and place where the buyer is to receive the goods. This is true even where "the place of shipment is the place of delivery." Thus, if the buyer picks the goods up and receives them at the seller's location that is the place where payment is due. In a "destination" contract, where delivery to the buyer will occur at the buyer's location, payment is due when the goods are delivered to the buyer at that place. In a "shipment" contract, where the goods will be tendered first to a carrier at the point of shipment and then delivered to the buyer by the carrier, payment is due when the goods are delivered to the buyer.

      1) **Delivery By Tender of Documents.** Where documents of title will be used to tender delivery, payment is due at the time and place where the documents are to be received by the buyer, regardless of where the goods will be delivered.

   Example: Contract provides a term of "$12,000, F.O.B. Seller's factory". Seller refuses to deliver the goods to a carrier for shipment to Buyer unless Buyer makes payment before their delivery to the carrier at Seller's factory. Seller has wrongfully refused to perform, as payment is not due until Buyer receives the goods at his location, even though the F.O.B. term is a shipment contract and even though the risk of loss passes to Buyer when the goods are delivered to the carrier.

   Example: Contract provides a term of "$7,000, C.I.F., Buyer's warehouse, Pittsburgh." "C.I.F." is a mercantile term indicating that payment is to be made against documents. Thus, payment is due when the documents are presented to the buyer, regardless of where and when the goods are to be received by the buyer.

   b. Method of Payment. Payment may be made by check or other method used in the ordinary course of business (such as a credit card). However, the seller may demand payment in currency if the seller gives the buyer any reasonably necessary extension of time to obtain the cash. When payment against documents is required, payment must be made when the documents are presented. Payment might also be made by a bank, on behalf of the buyer, pursuant to a Letter of Credit issued in favor of the seller, at the request of the buyer.

   Example: Seller delivers the goods to Buyer directly, using Seller's delivery truck. Buyer tenders payment via check, which Seller's truck driver refuses, demanding cash. Seller must give Buyer a further reasonable time to obtain the necessary cash before treating Buyer as being in breach.

5. **Buyer's Right To Reject: Perfect Tender Rule.** In contracts calling for a single delivery, UCC 2-601 retains the so-called "perfect tender rule" permitting a buyer to reject goods if there is any nonconformity in the goods or their tender. Where there is a nonconformity "in any respect" the buyer has the right to reject the whole, accept the whole, or accept any commercial unit or units and reject the rest.

   a. The right to reject is subject to any contractual limitation on the buyer's remedies under UCC 2-718 and to the seller's right under UCC 2-508 to cure.

   b. The perfect tender rule applies only to "single delivery" contracts and not to contracts permitting installment deliveries.

6. **Manner of Rejection**. Rejection consists of timely notification by the buyer that the buyer is rejecting the goods. Notification of Rejection must be made within a reasonable time after delivery or tender of the goods by the seller. Mere notice of a defect or nonconformity is not sufficient for notice of rejection. To reject, buyer must notify seller that buyer is refusing to accept or pay for goods due to the nonconformity.

   a. **Particularization of Defects**. Buyer must specify the grounds for a rejection and is estopped from relying on unstated defects to either justify rejection or to establish breach in situations where the seller could have cured the defect or, in a contract between merchants, where the seller, following rejection, has made a request in writing for a statement of all defects on which buyer proposes to rely.

7. **Revocation of Acceptance Due to Substantially Impairing Defect.** If the buyer has **accepted** the goods, the buyer may **revoke acceptance** and return the goods to the seller only if the defect is one that **substantially impairs the value of the goods to the contract.** This is the UCC equivalent of rescission due to material breach.

8. **Seller's Right To Cure under UCC 2-508.** When buyer rejects a non-conforming tender, the seller has a right to cure the defect in two situations: 1) where the non-conforming goods were delivered early and the time for performance is not yet due; or, 2) where the seller had reasonable grounds to believe goods would be acceptable to buyer.

   a. Seller must provide timely notice to buyer of its intent to cure.

9. **Buyer's Rights and Duties with Respect to Goods after Rejection or Revocation of Acceptance.**

   a. **Merchant Buyer's Duty to Follow Seller's Instructions Regarding Rejected Goods in Buyer's Possession.** If the buyer is a merchant, the buyer has a duty, after rejection, to follow any reasonable instructions received from the seller regarding disposition of the goods.

   b. **Buyer's Storage and Resale of Rejected Goods in Absence of Instructions from Seller**.

1) **Goods That Are Perishable or Otherwise Threaten to Decline Speedily in Value.** If the seller does not provide instructions, the **merchant buyer has a duty to make reasonable efforts to resell** any goods that are perishable or otherwise likely to decline speedily in value.

2) **Buyer's Right To Store and Resell Other Goods.** If the goods are not perishable and do not threaten to speedily decline in value, the buyer may store the rejected goods or may resell them on the seller's account. Any storage or resale does not constitute acceptance of the goods or conversion by the buyer. Resale by the buyer must be commercially reasonable and comply with the rules regarding resale by a breaching buyer in UCC 2-706.

3) **Buyer Has Right to Reimbursement for Expenses of Storage and Sale.** The buyer has a right to recover reimbursement for any expense incurred in storing or reselling the rejected goods.

c. **Buyer's Security Interest in Rejected Goods**. Where the buyer has made a down payment for rejected goods, the buyer has a security interest under UCC 2-711 in those goods to secure repayment of the buyer's down payment and recovery of any expenses incurred by the buyer in inspection, receipt, transportation, care custody, and resale of the goods.

10. **Installment Deliveries.** An "installment contract" exists where the seller is permitted or required to deliver the goods in separate lots, with acceptance to be made upon delivery of each lot. A contract permitting installment deliveries is an "installment contract" even if the agreement indicates that "each delivery is a separate contract" or other similar language.

a. **Substantial Impairment of Value of Single Installment.** In contracts providing for, or permitting delivery of the goods in installments, the perfect tender rule of UCC 2-601 does not apply. Instead, buyer may reject a delivery only if the nonconformity substantially impairs the value of the installment to the buyer or, for some reason, cannot be cured.

Example: Contract for the sale of 500,000 bricks for use in construction of a building in circumstances calling for always having sufficient bricks on hand for buyer's use. Because the circumstances permit delivery of less than all 500,000 bricks at once, the contract is an installment contract and the buyer may reject an installment only if the nonconformity substantially impairs the value of the installment to the buyer.

b. **Substantial Impairment of Entire Contract**. Where a non-conformity or default in one or more installments substantially impairs the value of the entire contract to the buyer, there is a breach of the entire contract permitting the buyer to exercise remedies for a breach of the whole, including cancellation.

11. **Timely Notice of Breach Required**. Where the buyer has accepted goods, the buyer must notify the seller of any breach within a reasonable time after the buyer discovers or should have discovered the breach **or be barred from any remedy**. Thus failure to provide timely notice prevents the buyer from obtaining any remedy, including revocation of acceptance or damages for breach of warranty. This supplements the rule that failure to timely notify seller of rejection constitutes acceptance.

F. FAIRNESS, GOOD FAITH, AND PUBLIC INTEREST; UNCONSCIONABLE CONTRACTS

1. **Duty of Good Faith and Fair Dealing**. Every contract includes an obligation of "good faith and fair dealing" in the performance of duties under the contract. The obligation of good faith prevents subterfuge and evasion. The obligation includes avoiding conduct that would prevent conditions from occurring or conduct that would hinder the other party's performance. Under some circumstances it includes a duty to engage in affirmative conduct to further the goal of performance of the contract between the parties.

   a. **UCC Duty of Good Faith**. UCC 1-203 imposes a general obligation of good faith in the performance or enforcement of every contract within the UCC. "Good faith" is defined in subjective terms as "**honesty in fact**" in the transaction. In the case of **merchants** in transactions under Article 2 a stricter standard of good faith applies. It requires "honesty in fact **and the observance of reasonable commercial standards of fair dealing in the trade."**

   b. **Good Faith in Requirements and Output Contracts.** In requirements and output contracts, where the quantity is measured by the buyer's requirements for the goods or the seller's production output of the goods, the requirements or output involved are those which occur in **good faith**. However, under UCC 2-306, the quantity may not be **unreasonably disproportionate** to any stated estimate or, if no estimate has been stated, to any normal or comparable prior requirements or output.

2. **Best Effort Obligation in Exclusive Dealing Contracts**. In other exclusive dealing contracts, such as for the sale of goods in a particular territory, or in real estate brokerage contracts, the party with the exclusive right has a duty to act in good faith and to use **best efforts** in marketing the goods or real estate subject to the exclusive dealing agreement.

3. **Termination and Acceleration at Will Provisions.** Long-term agreements for the sale of goods, or franchise agreements are sometimes subject to termination "at will" or "on notice" by one party. Other agreements, such as employment contracts or distributorship agreements, have no stated duration or notice requirement. Promissory notes and other financial obligations where payment is due in installments are sometimes subject to "acceleration" at will, requiring payment of the entire principal balance at once. These types of contracts are sometimes subject to a duty of good faith or reasonable notice before they may be terminated.

a. **Termination of Contracts for Sale of Goods under UCC 2-309.** Where a contract provides for successive performances, but does not state the duration of the agreement, the contract will be valid for a reasonable time, but may be terminated under UCC 2-309 at any time by either party. The termination requires **reasonable notification.**

b. **Franchise Agreements.** Some courts and state legislatures have imposed a duty of good faith and fair dealing requiring franchisors to continue a franchise agreement for a sufficiently long time to permit the franchisee to recoup its investment. Other courts have imposed no such obligation, permitting the agreement to be terminated completely at will if the contract does not express a contrary rule.

c. **Good faith** is required for a creditor to exercise an "acceleration at will" provision in a promissory note or other financial obligation. However, a promissory note requiring payment "on demand" is **not** subject to this obligation of good faith.

d. **At Will Employment**. Employment contracts are generally "at will," unless there is an express agreement for employment for a specific time or a clause stating that the employee will only be fired "for cause."

4. Unconscionable Contract or Terms

a. **Generally:** The court will refuse to enforce a contract or terms in a contract that are **unconscionable**. Unconscionability will be found when there was an **absence of meaningful choice** on the part of the party seeking to avoid the unconscionable provision and the terms are **unreasonably favorable to the other party.**

b. UCC 2-302 permits the court to refuse to enforce an unconscionable contract or an unconscionable term in order to **prevent oppression and unfair surprise**. As indicated below, a determination of unconscionability under UCC 2-302 results from a finding of both **procedural** and **substantive unconscionability.** Under UCC 2-302, the court must evaluate an allegedly unconscionable contract or term in light of the **commercial setting, purpose, and effect** of the contract.

VII. DISCHARGE OF CONTRACTS

A. DISCHARGE BY PERFORMANCE

The most common method for the discharge of contractual obligations is by performance.

B. RELEASE, RESCISSION, OR CONTRACT NOT TO SUE

A contract may usually be discharged by agreement between the parties. The requirements are the same as for any contract – there must be mutual assent and consideration.

1. **Rescission**. When the parties agree to rescind their agreement, the consideration for the agreement is the release of each party's respective duties to one another under the terms

of the initial contract. Any agreement between the parties which terminates their respective obligations to one another will qualify as a rescission, regardless of whether the parties use the term "rescission."

2. **Release** is usually used in connection with tort claims, but might just as easily refer to a voluntary agreement to release a person from his or her obligation to perform a contract. To be effective, the release must be supported by consideration, which will usually consist of each party's agreement to release the other from any remaining contractual duties. Where consideration is absent, reliance will also suffice.

3. The parties may also discharge their obligations by entering into a separate **contract not to sue**. A contract not to sue for any breach may be permanent, in which case the entire contract is discharged, or may only be temporary, which merely suspends the duties under the contract.

C. SUBSTITUTED PERFORMANCE OR SUBSTITUTED CONTRACT AND ACCORD AND SATISFACTION

1. The parties to a contract might enter into an agreement for a **substituted performance** or a **substituted contract** in which one performance or contract is substituted for a previously existing contract. This is essentially a modification of an existing contract and must be supported by **consideration**. So long as each party's performance is slightly different from that in the original contract, the substituted performance or contract is supported by consideration. A substituted performance or contract may be between the original parties or by a substitution of one of the obligors.

2. **Accord and Satisfaction.** Accord and satisfaction refers to situations where one of the parties is unwilling to give up whatever rights it may have under the parties' initial agreement until the other party has performed its obligation under the new arrangement. The new agreement is called an **accord,** and performance of the accord is a **satisfaction** (or discharge) of the original obligation. The obligor's duties under the original contract are not discharged until performance of the new agreement.

    a. **Distinguished from Substitute Contract.** In a **substitute contract,** the making of a new agreement discharges the parties' duties under the original agreement. In an **accord and satisfaction,** the original duties are not discharged until after performance of the second agreement. Despite the difference in precise meanings, "accord and satisfaction" is sometimes used to loosely refer to both types of transactions.

    b. **Effect of an Accord**. An accord **suspends** the original obligation. If an **accord** is breached, the obligee may choose to enforce either the accord or the original obligation.

c. **Consideration Required**. An accord and satisfaction requires consideration. Consideration is frequently a problem in this context because many accord and satisfactions involve only part performance of a pre-existing duty, such as where a person to whom payment is owed agrees to accept payment of a smaller sum as satisfaction of a larger debt.

1) **Bona Fide Dispute or Unliquidated Debt.** An accord and satisfaction discharges a pre-existing debt, even where a smaller sum is paid in satisfaction of a larger sum allegedly due, where there is some **bona fide dispute** over the enforceability or amount of the larger claim or where the amount of the debt is otherwise an **unliquidated sum.**

2) **Consideration Requirement Relaxed.** The consideration requirement has been eliminated in some jurisdictions, permitting release of a debt to pay an undisputed and unliquidated debt, on the payment of a lesser sum. Such a rule permits financially troubled debtors to settle their admitted debts by paying a portion of the amount owed, without the need for formal bankruptcy proceedings. In other jurisdictions the consideration requirement has been considerably relaxed, permitting any variation, no matter how slight, in the debtor's obligations, or sometimes permitting a written expression that consideration has been given, to make the settlement enforceable.

3) **Good Faith Modification of Contract for Sale or Lease of Goods**. UCC Articles 2 and 2A permit modification of contracts for the sale (Article 2) or lease (Article 2A) of goods *without consideration* where the modification was made in good faith.

D. "PAYMENT IN FULL" CHECK AS ACCORD AND SATISFACTION – EFFECT OF RESERVATION OF RIGHTS

Debtors sometimes attempt to pay a debt by sending a creditor a check marked "paid in full," anticipating that the creditor will cash the check and thus "accept" the offer to settle the debt.

1. **Pre-1990 UCC 1-207.** Under UCC 1-207, prior to the 1990 amendments, in most states a creditor's acceptance of a "payment in full" check was an accord and satisfaction of the underlying claim, even if the creditor qualified its indorsement by crossing out the "payment in full" language, by "reserving rights," or by some other manner which purported to preserve the creditor's claim on the unpaid portion of the debt.

2. **Post 1990 Revisions to UCC 1-207.** In 1990, UCC 1-207 was revised, adding language making it clear that it had no effect on an accord and satisfaction. At the same time, UCC 3-311 was added, providing a mechanism for determining whether cashing a "payment in full" check was an accord and satisfaction. Under UCC 3-311, a "payment in full" check can be used to effectuate an accord and satisfaction only where:

   a. the underlying claim is **unliquidated** or subject to a **bona fide dispute;**

b. the "payment in full" check is tendered **in good faith;**

c. the check contains or is accompanied by a **conspicuous statement** that the instrument was tendered as **full satisfaction of the claim;**

d. the **check is** deposited and **finally paid;** and

e. the check was either:

   1) **Sent to the specified address** of a creditor who is a corporation, partnership, or other **organization, who had previously sent notice to the debtor** advising it that communications concerning disputed debts, including checks intended as full payment, must be sent to that specified address;

   2) **Not refunded within 90 days after payment.** This alternative does not apply to a creditor who sent a notice to the debtor as indicated above; or

   3) The creditor or creditor's agent with direct responsibility for handling the disputed debt **knew that the check was tendered in full satisfaction of the claim.**

   Example: Consumer purchases auto from Dealer, borrowing the $25,000 purchase price from Bank. Consumer, who is completely satisfied with the car, sends check for $1,000, conspicuously marked "payment in full," to Bank which then cashes it marked "cashed under protest – rights reserved" and does not provide a refund. There is no accord and satisfaction because, although the Bank cashed a "payment in full" check, the debt is liquidated and there is no bona fide dispute about the debt.

   Example: Insurance Company sends auto accident Victim a check for $15,000 conspicuously marked "payment in full" and referring to the Victim's claim against the Insured. Victim cashes the check and does not provide a refund within 90 days. There has been a valid "accord and satisfaction." The claim was unliquidated, the check was sent in good faith and cashed, and no refund was provided.

   Example: Customer purchases furniture from Furniture Store, Inc., on credit. Store sends Customer notice that any communications regarding disputed debts, including any payments intended to fully satisfy any debt owed by the Customer, should be sent to a specific post office box address. Dissatisfied with the furniture because of defects, Customer sends a check, conspicuously marked as "payment in full," for 70% of the outstanding balance to the Store's street address, at the location from which the furniture was purchased. Store cashes the check. There is no valid "accord and satisfaction." Although the debt was the subject of a bona fide dispute, the Store is an organization and Customer had received Store's previously sent notice of the address to which settlement checks should be sent but, nevertheless, sent it to a different address.

a) **Performance or Acceptance under Reservation of Rights under UCC 1-207.** A party who continues performance or promises continued performance, or who agrees to accept a performance proposed by the other party, does not prejudice its rights for any earlier breach or waive any alleged breach if it explicitly reserves its rights or indicates that it is continuing with performance "under protest" or via other language that indicates that its continued performance or acceptance of continued performance by the other party is not a waiver. This rule is intended to encourage parties to continue performance of a contract despite the presence of a continued dispute over past or continued performance. Any other rule would discourage continued performance pending resolution of the parties' dispute. This rule does not apply to situations where performance is complete and there is an alleged "accord and satisfaction."

Example: Seller tenders delivery of defective goods under contract providing for installment deliveries. Buyer accepts defective goods but gives notice of the nonconformity and advises Seller that it will continue to accept goods but that it "reserves rights" as to the harm caused by the defects. Buyer's willingness to accept the defective goods does not operate as a waiver of the defect.

E. DISCHARGE BY NOVATION

A novation occurs when the parties agree to substitute performance by a third party for the performance of one of the original parties to the contract. It is distinguished from a **delegation of duty** to a third party because the original party to the contract is **released** from the duty to perform. Consideration is provided by the agreement of the new party to perform the obligation of the party whose duties are released.

F. DISCHARGE BY EXCUSE

1. **Impossibility or Commercial Impracticability.** Duties under a contract can be excused due to an unanticipated change of circumstances that renders performance impossible or, under UCC 2-615, commercially impracticable.

a. **Traditional Impossibility Rule.** At common law, executory duties under a contract were excused where performance became impossible due to an unanticipated change of circumstances that was beyond the control of the parties. These cases were sometimes decided on the basis of the failure of some **implied condition** of the parties' duties under the contract. Contracts were excused due to impossibility in the following situations:

1) **Death or Disability.** Death or disability is an excuse only where the services were personal, so that another person could not perform the contract, such as

where a musician becomes deaf or an artist dies. Death or disability is an excuse where the life or capacity of a person was an **implied condition** of the contract.

2) **Destruction of the Subject Matter of the Contract.** Destruction of the subject matter of the contract, not caused by the party seeking to be relieved from performance, is also an excuse where the continued existence of the subject matter was necessary and thus an **implied condition.**

   Example: A contract for a musical performance specifies the theatre at which the performance will occur. Before the scheduled date for the performance the theatre burns down, without the fault of either party. Because the continued existence of the theatre was an implied condition of the contract, the parties' duties are excused.

   a) **Contracts for Sale of Land - Destruction of a Structure.** In contracts for the sale of real estate, where a structure on the realty is destroyed before closing and delivery of a deed, performance will not be excused, because it is **not impossible**; the buyer can still pay and the seller can still deliver a deed. In such cases, however, the purchase price may be abated to the extent of the seller's insurance coverage.

   b) **Construction Contracts.** In cases involving destruction of a partially completed building, courts distinguish between new construction and repair or renovation.
      i) **New Construction.** In cases involving new construction, performance by the builder is not excused, because performance is not impossible and the risk of destruction prior to completion is considered to rest upon the builder.

      ii) **Repair or Renovation.** In cases involving repair or renovation, performance by the builder and the owner is excused. The owner will be obligated to pay the builder, on a theory of restitution, for the value of improvements incorporated into the structure before it was destroyed.

      Example: Contract between Builder and Owner for construction of new hockey stadium on Owner's land. After 2/3 completion of the stadium and installation of a roof, a heavy unprecedented snowstorm causes the completed roof to collapse. Builder is not excused from performance and is not entitled to extra compensation for fixing the collapsed roof.

      Example: In a contract between Builder and Owner for installation of an addition to Owner's home, the home, including the partially completed addition, is destroyed in a tornado. Both Builder and Owner are excused from further performance, but Owner must pay Builder for the value of improvements made before the tornado.

c) **Casualty To Identified Goods.** This aspect of the traditional impossibility doctrine is codified in UCC 2-613 which excuses the seller from performing where **goods identified to the contract *at the time it was made*** are destroyed before tender of delivery and without the fault of either party. This rule frequently applies to contracts for the sale of crops grown on a specific parcel of land where the crops are destroyed before harvest. This rule only applies where the contract was for the sale of specific items selected and identified at the time the contract was made. It does not apply when the specific goods to be delivered under the contract are identified some time after the contract was entered into.

Example: Buyer and Seller enter into a contract for the sale of a specific "floor model" of a dining room table on display in the Seller's showroom. Before delivery, the goods are destroyed by a tornado. Because the specific table was selected and identified at the time the contract was made, and the goods were destroyed before delivery due to circumstances beyond control of the parties, the Seller is excused from its duty to deliver the goods under UCC 2-613.

Example: Buyer examined furniture on display in store and made a contract to purchase a sofa like the one on display in Seller's store, with the understanding that an identical item would be delivered to Buyer from Seller's inventory. The day after the contract was made, Seller selected a sofa from its inventory and marked it for delivery to the Buyer, thus identifying the goods to the contract. Later that day, and before delivery, a flood destroyed Seller's warehouse and all of the inventory it contained, including its supply of sofas like the one Seller had promised to deliver. The Seller is not excused under UCC 2-613 or the traditional doctrine of impossibility because the goods were not identified to the contract **when it was made**. Identification to the contract occurred later and existence of the specific goods was not an implied condition of the Seller's duty to perform. The doctrine of commercial impracticability may, however, excuse the seller, depending on the difficulty of performance after the flood.

3) **Supervening Illegality.** Where the parties have made a contract on the assumption that performance of the contract would continue to be legal, a subsequent decision of a court or an act of the legislature making the contract illegal will excuse performance of the contract.

Example: Casino hires Dealer to work at the Casino's blackjack tables for a year. Subsequently, the legislature outlaws gambling. The parties' duties under the contract are excused.

b. **No Excuse where Party Seeking Relief Assumed the Risk of Loss**. Impossibility is not an excuse where, under the terms of the contract, the party seeking relief has assumed the risk of loss or the risk of the intervening event which occasioned the loss.

1) **Risk of Loss in Contracts for the Sale of Goods.** In contracts for the sale of goods the risk of loss passes from the seller to the buyer:

   a) in cases involving shipment by a carrier when either the goods are provided to the carrier in a **shipment contract**; or when they are tendered by the carrier to the buyer in a **destination contract.** Whether the contract is a shipment or destination contract depends on whether the **F.O.B.** term indicates a place of shipment or destination.

   b) in cases where the goods are in storage with an independent warehouse, when the documents or title necessary for their release to the buyer are tendered to the buyer or when the warehouseman acknowledges the buyer's right to possession of the goods.

   c) in other cases the risk of loss passes to the buyer upon the seller's tender of delivery, or **if the seller is a merchant**, upon the buyer's receipt of the goods.

2) **Effect of Breach on Risk of Loss.** Breach by the buyer or seller can affect the risk of loss.

   a) **Non-Conforming Goods.** If the **buyer has not accepted** nonconforming goods, the risk of loss remains on the seller until cure by the seller or acceptance by the buyer. If defective goods are destroyed **after the buyer justifiably revokes acceptance** the buyer may treat the risk of loss as remaining on the seller to the extent of any deficiency in the buyer's insurance coverage.

   b) **Breach or Repudiation by the Buyer before Risk of Loss Passes**. If the buyer repudiates or commits some other breach before the risk of loss has passed to the buyer, the seller may, for a reasonable time, treat the risk of loss as resting on the buyer to the extent of any deficiency in the seller's insurance coverage.

Watch Out!

A favorite fact pattern of bar examiners involves the destruction of the subject matter of a contract. Typically, in this type of fact pattern, you will see a deal involving the sale of goods. Before the buyer receives these goods, something will cause them to be destroyed. The buyer will sue. Whether the buyer can recover will depend on whether the risk of loss has shifted from the seller to the buyer.

c. **Modern Doctrine of Commercial Impracticability**. The modern doctrine of commercial impracticability is codified in UCC 2-615. It excuses the parties from continued performance of a contract where all of the following apply:

1) **performance has become impossible or impracticable** without extremely undue difficulty or expense, not merely consisting of additional expense;

2) due to an **unanticipated event or circumstance**;

3) the **non-occurrence** of the intervening event was **a basic assumption of the parties.** The event must have been **not reasonably foreseeable** by the parties at the time the contract was made;

4) the **risk** of occurrence of the event was **not assumed** by the party seeking avoidance of the contract; and

5) the **event was not caused** by the party seeking avoidance of the contract.

d. **Partial Impossibility or Delay**. The doctrine of impossibility operates only to excuse partial non-performance or delay where the partial or late performance remains possible despite the occurrence of the unanticipated intervening event.

Example: In a construction contract, where unusual continued temperature extremes prevent timely completion of outdoor portions of a building, performance of the entire contract is not excused, but delay, to the extent that timely performance was rendered impossible, will be excused.

Watch Out!

Impossibility is only a valid defense if **all** of the following conditions are met:

- Performance is objectively impossible (nobody could perform the duties in accordance with the terms of the contract).
- Impossibility arises **after** formation of the contract.
- Performance is **completely** impossible (otherwise the duty will only be discharged for that portion which could not be performed).
- Performance is **permanently** impossible, not just temporarily (unless it places too great of a burden on one of the parties to justify continuation of the duty).
- If it is a service contract, it must be one for **unique services** that cannot be delegated to someone else.

2. **Frustration of Purpose.** Frustration of purpose excuses a party where, although performance is not impossible, unanticipated circumstances beyond the control of the party seeking relief has resulted in a complete frustration of the parties' purpose in

making the contract. It only applies where both parties contemplated the purpose of the contract at the time it was made. Frustration will excuse a party only where all of the following apply:

a. the contemplated **purpose of the contract would be frustrated;**

b. due to an **unanticipated event or circumstance**;

c. the **non-occurrence** of the intervening event was **a basic assumption of the contract.** The event must have been **not reasonably foreseeable** by the parties at the time the contract was made;

d. the **risk** of occurrence of the event was **not assumed** by the party seeking avoidance of the contract; and

e. the frustrating **event** was **not caused by the party seeking avoidance** of the contract.

3. **Mistake.** Parties are also excused when the contract was entered into based on a mutual mistake of fact that was a basic assumption of the parties to the contract.

   a. Excuse based on mutual mistake requires:

      1) **mutual mistake by both parties** to the contract; if only one party was mistaken it is merely a unilateral mistake for which relief is more difficult;

      2) **of a material fact,** and not a mere opinion related to the anticipated value of the contract. A mere mistake about the anticipated or actual value of the promised performance, or a mistaken judgment, is not grounds for excuse due to mistake. A mutual mistake about the legality of an agreement, however, is a mistake which entitles the parties to relief;

      3) the mistake must have a **material effect** on the parties' exchange. A mistake about a minor matter that has no substantial or material impact on the exchange will not justify relief;

      4) the mistaken fact must have been **about a basic assumption** of the contract;

      5) the party seeking the excuse must not have assumed the risk of the mistake. Courts will sometimes evaluate the relative expertise of the parties and allocate the risk of a mistake to the party who was in the best position to have taken steps to avoid the mistake. In other situations, the court will place the risk on a party who agreed to a contract despite his conscious uncertainty about the true facts.

b. **Mutual Mistake in Particular Circumstances.**

1) **Sale of Goods.** Mutual mistake in cases involving sales of goods usually involves a mistake about the nature of the thing involved, such as a valuable jewel mistakenly believed to be nothing more than a pretty rock, or a valuable coin, mistakenly believed to be worth no more than its face value. In such cases the issue is usually whether the party seeking relief has **assumed the risk** of the mistaken fact, particularly where the parties have entered into the contract conscious of the uncertainty of the true facts. When the parties make a contract in the face of **known uncertainty,** relief based on mistake is not available. However, where the parties are not conscious of the risk of mistake, relief will be granted.

Example: Buyer and Seller enter into a contract for the sale of an antique stock certificate for $20, reasonably believed by both parties to be worth nothing more than its historic or aesthetic value and not representing ownership of an equity interest in an existing corporation. After the contract is made, the parties discover that ownership of the certificate represents ownership of shares in an existing corporation worth $100,000. The mutual mistake of the parties was a mistake about the nature of the thing itself.

2) **Construction Contracts.** Relief due to mistake is unlikely to be granted in construction contracts where the parties have entered into the contract based on a false and mistaken assumption about underground conditions. The builder is likely to be treated as having **assumed the risk** of these conditions; however, where the parties conducted reasonable testing to determine the conditions, and the results of the testing proved unreliable, a court might decide that the risk should remain on the owner of the land and excuse the builder.

c. **Unilateral Mistake**. Unilateral mistake by one party to the contract is not usually grounds for excuse. A few cases provide relief based on a unilateral mistake where the mistake was discovered before the other party reasonably relied on the mistake – as where a contractor discovers and reports a clerical error in a bid shortly after it has been accepted and where other bidders are still available to enter into the contract.

1) **Snap-up of mistaken offer prohibited.** Relief will also be provided where a party "snaps up" an offer with reason to know that it was made pursuant to some unilateral mistake or clerical error.

VIII. UNENFORCEABILITY ON GROUNDS OF PUBLIC POLICY OR UNCONSCIONABILITY

A. ILLEGALITY

Contracts for an illegal or criminal purpose are not enforceable. Restitution is not available for benefits rendered under a criminally illegal contract. Examples of illegal contracts include contracts in restraint of trade, contracts to pay a usurious rate of interest on a loan, contracts to commit a crime, conspiracies or other agreements to obstruct justice, and gambling contracts.

1. **Contract to Commit Crime.** An agreement to commit a crime is unenforceable. This includes price-fixing agreements in violation of Federal Antitrust laws, murders for hire, criminal conspiracies, promises to pay a bribe to a public official or engage in any other conduct which is subject to criminal sanction.

2. **Contract to Commit a Tort or Breach of Fiduciary Duty.** An agreement to participate in some tortious behavior or conduct is unenforceable as violative of public policy.

3. **Contract Made Without Valid Business License.** Contracts entered into by parties who lack a necessary business license may be illegal, as in violation of public policy, where the licensing requirement has been imposed to ensure the quality of service provided by the provider. Where the contract is unenforceable, recovery in restitution is usually not available. However, where the license is required merely as a means of generating revenue, the contract is enforceable.

   Example: Contract to provide legal services by person not admitted to the bar is unenforceable. An unlicensed law school graduate will not be able to obtain restitution for value of services provided.

   Example: A Furniture Store enters into contract to sell Sofa and Chairs after expiration of its business license. Business licenses are given to anyone who pays the applicable fee. The contract is enforceable.

B. RESTRAINTS OF TRADE – COVENANTS NOT TO COMPETE

Agreements not to compete are legal and enforceable where they are **reasonable restraints** and **ancillary** to an otherwise legal contract or transaction.

1. **Ancillary To An Otherwise Legally Enforceable Contract.** Reasonable restrictions on a person's ability to compete with another are enforceable when they are **ancillary** to some other agreement such as an employment contract or an agreement for the sale of a business. They are appropriate to protect the employer's trade secrets or to enable the buyer of a business a reasonable opportunity to enjoy the value of the good will of a business she has purchased. A simple agreement providing for payment of money by one party to another in exchange for the other's promise not to compete, is not enforceable and is likely in violation of criminal antitrust laws.

2. **Restraint Must Be Reasonable.** A restraint on competition will be enforceable only to the extent that it is reasonable in geographic scope and duration. A covenant in an employment contract prohibiting the employee, upon voluntary termination, from ever working for anyone engaged in the same business as his employer in any location would, for example, be likely treated as unreasonable. To be reasonable, the restraint must be reasonably calculated to protect the legitimate interests of the promisee in the relevant geographic market and even then only for a reasonable time.

3. **Remedy for Unreasonable Restraint**. Where the non-compete provision is ancillary, but is unreasonably broad in scope or duration a court may simply strike the provision from the contract or may exercise its equitable powers to limit its scope or duration to a reasonable extent. The former approach encourages parties to draft reasonable restraints while the latter approach implements the legitimate purposes of the underlying contract.

   Example: Retiring Dentist enters into contract to sell his downtown dentistry practice, including goodwill, to a recent dental school Graduate. The contract prohibits Retiring Dentist from engaging in the practice of dental medicine anywhere in the state for a period of 10 years. The restraint, though ancillary to the sale of the business, covers too broad a geographic area and is for too lengthy a duration. Protection of the recent Graduate's purchase of Retiring Dentist's good will does not reasonably require preventing her from practicing anywhere in the state, or even from resuming practice in the downtown area after a reasonable period of several years.

C. INCAPACITY OF THE PARTIES

Contracts entered into by parties who lack mental capacity to make a voluntary agreement are not enforceable. Capacity may be lacking due to age, mental impairment, duress, undue influence, or fraud.

1. **Disaffirmance.** A party seeking to avoid a contract due to incapacity must "disaffirm" the contract. Any such disaffirmance must occur within a reasonable time after the incapacity is removed, such as by reaching the age of majority or the recovery of mental capacity to contract. Further, a person who takes advantage of the benefits of the contract, after removal of the incapacity, will be found to have **affirmed or "ratified"** the contract and will be bound by it. Silence in use of the benefits of the contract, after expiration of the disability, may therefore constitute ratification of the contract.

2. **Effect of Incapacity.** When a contract is unenforceable due to incapacity, the party seeking relief will be required to provide restitution of the benefits remaining in its possession, and in some limited situations may be required, as a condition of disaffirmance, to provide restitution for all benefits previously received from the other party. Likewise, a person may be liable **in restitution** for any **necessities of life** such as food, clothing, and shelter, received under a contract made while lacking capacity.

3. **Infancy.** A person under the age of 18, the age of majority in American jurisdictions, lacks capacity to make a contract and can disaffirm the contract within a reasonable time after reaching the age of majority.

a. **Restitution of Remaining Benefits**. To disaffirm, a minor must provide restitution of any benefits remaining in his possession, but need not provide restitution of benefits used or consumed prior to his or her disaffirmance. In some jurisdictions a minor who seeks not just to avoid continued performance, but to recoup any consideration paid to the other party, is liable for the value of any benefits received under the contract prior to his or her attempt to disaffirm.

b. **Necessaries of Life**. A minor must make full restitution for the value of any necessaries of life received pursuant to the disaffirmed contract. Necessaries include food, shelter, clothing, and non-elective medical care.

c. **Misrepresentation of Age**. A minor who enters into the contract by misrepresenting his age may be prevented from disaffirming due to fraud, if reliance on the misrepresentation was reasonable.

4. **Mental Incapacity.** Mental incapacity is treated similar to infancy. The person suffering the mental incapacity must disaffirm within a reasonable time after reacquiring his or her mental ability. The person is liable in restitution for the value of any necessaries received while suffering from the debilitating condition. Some jurisdictions require restitution for the value of all benefits received during the mental incapacity. The principal difficulty is in determining the circumstances that constitute mental incapacity.

a. **Inability To Understand Test**. The traditional test for mental incapacity is whether the person has sufficient mental ability to understand the nature and consequences of the agreement. Under this test it does not matter if the other party to the contract knew or had reason to know of the disabled person's lack of capacity.

b. **Inability To Control Actions Test.** A more liberal test depends on whether, due to a mental illness or disease, the person lacks the ability to control his or her actions, even though he might have the ability to understand the nature and consequences of the contract. Courts applying this test require that the other party to the contract **have reason to know** of the disability, in order for it to apply.

c. **Court Adjudication of Incapacity**. Contracts entered into by a person who has been adjudicated to lack mental capacity and had a guardian appointed are not enforceable. The adjudication creates at least a presumption of lack of mental capacity and in many jurisdictions is conclusive.

d. **Drugs and Alcohol**. Contracts entered into under the influence of mind altering drugs or intoxicating alcohol may be disaffirmed only if the intoxicated person lacked the ability to understand the nature of the transaction and the other person had reason to know of his disability.

5. **Duress**. Physical duress deprives a person of the ability to consent to a contract. Contracts entered into under duress are not enforceable. Duress consists of an improper threat that induces the victim's expression of agreement and which is grave enough to

leave the victim with no reasonable alternative other than to express consent. Duress usually consists of a threat of physical harm, either to the person whose assent is sought or to some other person. It might consist of a threat of criminal investigation, which, even if warranted on the facts, is improper if used for private gain. A threat to break a contract is not usually sufficiently grave to constitute duress, but might qualify as economic duress, discussed below. A threat to sue on the basis of some legitimate claim is not enough.

6. **Undue Influence.** Undue influence can also render a contract unenforceable. Undue influence consists of **improper or unfair persuasion** by a person in **a relationship of confidence or trust** with the person whose consent is obtained.

   a. **Improper or Unfair Persuasion** exists when threats or unrelenting persuasion is used, particularly with respect to a person in a weakened or vulnerable situation.

   b. **Relationship of Trust or Confidence** exists when there is some special relationship between the parties, such as husband-wife, clergy-communicant, physician-patient, lawyer-client, or other relationship where one person places particular trust in the other. It might also exist where there is some sort of dominant-subservient relationship between the parties, perhaps induced by the weakened condition of one of the parties.

   Example: The agreement of a school teacher persuaded to resign by the school principal after his arrest and a full day of police questioning about his alleged criminal activity was not enforceable due to misuse of weakened and emotional condition of the teacher by a the principal in a dominant position over the teacher.

7. **Economic Duress**. Economic duress has been used to make agreements to modify contracts unenforceable where the party who agreed to the modification has no realistic economic alternative but to accede to the demands for modification of the other party. The unavailability of an economic substitute and the impracticality of seeking equitable relief for a threatened breach of contract makes relief on the grounds of economic duress likely.

   Example: Modification obtained by offshore Alaskan fisherman who induced employer to agree to increased wages after ship was at sea where returning to shore to find replacements would mean abandoning the fishing season entirely was unenforceable due to economic duress.

D. FRAUD, LACK OF GOOD FAITH, AND UNCONSCIONABILITY

1. **Fraud and Misrepresentation.** Fraud is a tort based on a false representation of a material fact that is reasonably relied upon to the other person's detriment.

a. **Omission of a Material Fact** can also constitute fraud, as where the seller of a house intentionally fails to tell the buyer of an adverse condition, known to the seller, which materially affects the value of the house.

2. **Duty of Good Faith, Best Efforts, and Fair Dealing.** Contracts include a general obligation of good faith and fair dealing in their performance.

a. **Meaning of Good Faith**. In contracts for the sale or lease of goods, governed by the UCC, **good faith** means **honesty in fact** in the conduct or transaction involved. UCC 1-201(19). In situations involving **merchants**, good faith means **both honesty in fact and observance of reasonable commercial standards of fair dealing in the trade.** UCC 2-103(1)(b).

b. **Duty of Good Faith in Specific Situations.** The duty of good faith and fair dealing applies to every contract but has its greatest impact in the following situations:

1) **Requirements and Output Contracts**. Under UCC 2-306, the quantity of goods to be purchased under a requirements contract and the quantity of goods to be sold under an output contract is determined with reference to **good faith requirements** of the buyer and **good faith output** of the seller.

2) **Other Exclusive Dealing Contracts**, giving one of the parties the exclusive rights to sell or buy certain goods in a particular territory or otherwise, imposes on the party with exclusive rights the obligation to use its **best efforts** to sell and promote the goods or services involved.

3) **Percentage Leases** which measure the landlord's rent based on a percentage of the lessee's sales, like exclusive dealing contracts, impose an obligation on the lessee to use its **best efforts** to generate sales.

4) **Franchise Agreements** and other contracts that are subject to **termination at will** are frequently interpreted to impose an obligation to exercise the termination provision **in good faith** and in observation of **reasonable standards of fair dealing in the trade.**

5) **Other Contracts Involving a Condition of Satisfaction.** Where a contract is subject to a condition of satisfaction, it means the **good faith** satisfaction of the party and does not permit a party to feign dissatisfaction with performance for reasons unrelated to the quality or satisfactory character of the performance.

6) **Modifications To Contracts.** Traditional rules required consideration for a contract to be modified. UCC 2-209 permits enforceability of any **good faith** modification to a contract for the sale of goods. Restatement 2d § 89 allows a modification which is **fair and equitable** in view of a change in circumstances not anticipated by the parties when the contract was made enforceable.

3. **Unconscionability**. The doctrine of unconscionability makes contracts or more often individual terms of contracts unenforceable when the contract or term is unusually **one sided or unfair**, usually combined with a **disparity in bargaining position between the parties** at the time the contract was made.

   a. **History of Unconscionability as Equitable Doctrine**. Unconscionability was originally a doctrine applied by a court of equity which **refused to specifically enforce** contracts or terms that were unusually **harsh or one-sided** or where the impact of enforcement would have an unusually harsh impact on a party who **lacked bargaining power** at the time the contract was made.

   b. **Unconscionability under UCC 2-302.** The modern doctrine of unconscionability is represented by UCC 2-302, though the doctrine applies to all types of contracts, not just contracts for the sale of goods. UCC 2-302 permits a court to refuse to enforce any contract or any clause in a contract that was **unconscionable at the time the contract was made** or if enforcement of the contract or provision would lead to an **unconscionable result**.

   c. **Meaning of Unconscionability: Oppression and Unfair Surprise.** The official comments to UCC 2-302 indicate that the unconscionability doctrine is designed to **prevent oppression and unfair surprise.** This has been interpreted as involving two separate aspects: **substantive and procedural unconscionability.** Contracts that have been held to be unconscionable have almost always involved some aspects of both substantive and procedural unconscionability.

      1) **Substantive Unconscionability.** Substantive unconscionability refers to the substantive unfairness of the terms of the contract. Terms are characterized as oppressive and therefore unconscionable when they are **unduly one-sided** with no corresponding benefit to the other party, or where provisions that are not called to the attention of a party go **beyond the reasonable expectations** that a party had in making the agreement. Examples of terms that have been treated as oppressive or substantively unconscionable are:

         a) **Limited remedy provisions** in contracts for defective consumer goods that **exclude liability for personal injury**, such as the one found in ***Henningsen v. Bloomfield Motors***, 32 N.J. 358, 161 A.2d 69 (1960), where a term appearing on the back of a detailed two-page contract, purporting to limit liability for breach of warranty to replacement of defective parts for 90 days or 4,000 miles, and excluding liability for any personal injury, was held unenforceable.

         b) **Cross-collateralization clauses** of the type found in the decision of ***Williams v. Walker-Thomas Furniture Co.***, 350 F.2d 445 (D.C. Cir. 1965), permitting a furniture dealer to repossess all items purchased by a customer over a long period of time, despite customer having paid the price for all but the most recently purchased item.

c) **Unconscionably High Price.** Courts have been reluctant to hold even exorbitantly high prices unconscionable, such as where a person has agreed to pay $1000 for a washing machine worth no more than $200, in the absence of hidden costs which raised the price without fair notice or some other type of unfair surprise about the price. In such cases the critical element of procedural unconscionability is usually missing because the buyer was not surprised about the price but knew what it was.

2) **Procedural Unconscionability.** Procedural unconscionability refers to some procedural unfairness in the formation of the contract that might even lead the court to conclude that mutual assent was absent. This aspect of unconscionability is usually described in terms of **unfair surprise,** an **unfair disparity in the bargaining power between the parties**, or, an **absence of meaningful choice.** Examples of situations involving procedural unconscionability include:

a) **Inconspicuous Limited Remedy Provisions.** Although UCC 2-719 does not explicitly require that limited remedy provisions be conspicuous in order to be enforceable, courts have imposed this requirement to prevent unconscionable unfair surprise.

b) **Limited liability language** in a parking lot receipt exculpating the parking lot operator from any responsibility for damage to the car or its contents where there was no meaningful opportunity to negotiate the one-sided terms of the agreement.

c) **Indemnification Provisions** in gas filling station distributorship contracts imposing liability on operator of filling station for negligence of gas company employees where the provision was **not called to the attention** of the filling station operator.

d) **Adhesion Contracts**. Adhesion contracts are those in which one of the parties is presented with the contract on a **take-it-or-leave-it basis** with no opportunity to negotiate or vary the terms of the contract. Although many unconscionability cases involve adhesion contracts, particularly in consumer settings, **most adhesion contracts are enforceable**. Examples are **insurance policies** and **installment sales agreements** which are enforceable so long as they **do not contain unusually one-sided terms** which are not called to the attention of the other party.

d. **Consumer and Business Situations.** Most unconscionability cases have involved transactions with consumers. However, the unconscionability doctrine has not been limited to consumer cases. Courts have used unconscionability in a variety of business settings, but particularly in franchise and distributorship agreements where there is a disparity of bargaining position between the parties.

e. **Role of the Court.** Determinations about unconscionability are made by the court as a matter of law. However, UCC 2-302 specifies that, before a determination about unconscionability can be made, the parties must be provided with an opportunity for an **evidentiary hearing** before the judge on the **commercial setting, purpose, and effect** of the contract or provision in question. Courts should not make determinations that a contract is unconscionable without giving the parties this opportunity.

f. **Consequences of Determination of Unconscionability.** If the court determines that a contract is unconscionable, it may **refuse to enforce the contract** at all, may enforce the contract **without the unconscionable term** or may **limit the application** of the unconscionable provision to **avoid any unconscionable result.**

IX. REMEDIES FOR BREACH OF CONTRACT

A. EXPECTATION, RELIANCE AND RESTITUTION DAMAGES

Contract damages are based on one of three basic remedial goals of contract law: ***expectation, reliance, and restitution.*** Expectation damages are used unless there is a reason to use the reliance or restitution alternatives. There are several standard **expectation remedies** that apply to recurring situations in contracts for construction, for the sale of goods, for employment, and for real estate contracts. All contract damages are subject to three important limitations: foreseeability, reasonable certainty, and mitigation (avoidability). In addition, a plaintiff must show that the breach proximately caused the harm. Showing causation is usually straightforward.

1. **Expectation Interest.** The basic goal of contract damages is to place the innocent party in as good a position as it would have been in had the contract been performed, usually through an award of money damages. Compensation should be based on lost expectations.

   a. **UCC 1-106.** Remedies in the UCC are to be liberally administered in pursuit of the goal of compensating for lost expectations by placing the aggrieved party in as good a position as performance.

   b. **Expectation Damages** are usually measured by the **lost value** of performance plus other or consequential loss, but less expenses saved as a result of the breach and less any losses avoided as a result of the breach. Damages for lost value and consequential loss are limited by the requirements of the doctrines of foreseeability, certainty, and mitigation (avoidability).

   c. **Expectation Damage Formulas**. Standard expectation damage formulas are normally used to compute damages for breach of contract. These standard formulas apply to most commonly recurring circumstances.

d. **Equitable Remedies**, such as specific performance and injunctions, are available only when the legal remedy of monetary compensation is inadequate and a balance of the equities favors relief.

2. **Reliance Interest.** An alternative goal of contract remedies seeks to restore the innocent party to the position it would have been in if the contract had not been made. This is usually accomplished by awarding damages based on the innocent party's out-of-pocket expenses incurred in connection with the contract. Reliance damages are also subject to the requirements of the doctrines of foreseeability, reasonable certainty, mitigation (avoidability), and causation.

    a. **Reliance** is frequently used when expectation damages are unavailable due to the requirement that damages be reasonably certain. When expectation damages are speculative, expenses incurred in reliance on the contract is an alternative recovery.

    b. Damages are also based on reliance when there is no formal contract, but the promisee has relied to his detriment on the express or implied promises of the defendant.

3. **Restitution Interest.** The restitution interest seeks to prevent unjust enrichment by awarding the value of any benefit conferred due to partial performance prior to the breach or other termination of the contract. Restitution is utilized not just as a remedy for breach of contract, but as a remedy for a breaching party who has conferred a substantial benefit prior to his breach. It is also used in quasi-contract where parties have conferred benefits on one another in the absence of an enforceable contract or where performance of a contractual obligation is excused due to mistake, impossibility, or other excuse.

B. EMPLOYMENT CONTRACTS

1. **Breach by the Employee.** Employer may recover for the cost of performance the additional amount the employer must incur to hire a substitute for the breaching employee. The employee will usually be entitled to recover for the value of any work done prior to the breach, in quasi contract, to prevent a penalty.

2. **Breach by the Employer.** The employee can recover the salary due for the term of employment, offset by any compensation the employee receives from an alternative job taken in mitigation of damages.

    a. **Mitigation.** Employee has a duty to make reasonable efforts to seek and accept substantially similar employment in an effort to mitigate damages. An employee who turns down substantially similar employment will have the amount that would have been earned from the similar employment deducted from his or her claim for the wages due from the breaching employer.

    Example: Movie Production Company terminates employment agreement with Actress to perform the starring role in a singing and dancing movie in which Actress was to have control over the script. She rejected an offer of alternative employment in a dramatic western movie, without control over the script. The amount she would have earned in the alternative movie is not deducted from her recovery of the agreed salary because a dramatic role without control over the script in a "western" movie was not substantially similar to a role in a singing-dancing movie in which the actress would have control over the script.

1) Unemployment compensation is not deducted from wages that would have been earned.

b. **Employment at Will.** An employer's unilateral termination of an "employment at will" contract is not a breach of contract; there is only a breach where the agreement was for a set term or until a specific job was completed.

C. CONSTRUCTION CONTRACTS

1. **Owner or Recipient's Damages - Breach by the Contractor**. Where an employee, contractor, or other provider of services breaches, the standard damage formula is based on either the **Cost of Performance or the Difference in Value**, together with any damages for foreseeable consequential harm and minus any expenses saved or losses avoided as a result of the breach.

a. **Cost of Performance**. Damages are usually based on the cost, above and beyond the agreed contract price, of obtaining the same services from another provider. Note that the concept of mitigation applies to the selection of the replacement provider.

1) **Restitution Recovery by Breaching Party.** The breaching contractor will be entitled to recover, in quasi-contract, for the value of the work performed before breach, offset by the owner's damages in the additional cost to complete the work.

Example: Carousel Owner hired Craftsman to restore 30 historic carousel horses for a price of $30,000. Craftsman breached without ever beginning work. The cheapest price anyone else would take for restoring the carousel horses was $36,000. The additional cost of $6,000 is Owner's basic recovery, together with the recovery of any down-payment Owner paid to Craftsman prior to his breach.

b. **The Difference in Value** between what was promised and what was received is used as an alternative where the cost of performance is grossly disproportionate to the value of the completed performance and would involve undue economic waste, or a windfall to the owner.

Example: Contractor agrees to construct a house for Owner using "Reading" pipe. Contractor completes the house with "Cohoes" pipe, which is of the same grade as "Reading" but is not from the same manufacturer. The cost of performance would be the equivalent of tearing the house down and rebuilding it with Reading pipe, though the value of the house, as constructed, is the same as it would have been had the

"Reading" pipe been used. The Owner will be limited to the difference in value between the house as promised and as built by Contractor, probably resulting in only nominal damages.

1) **Cost of Performance** will be used, even if it is disproportionate to the difference in value, where cost of performance is **necessary to fulfill an aesthetic or individualistic value** of the innocent party.

   Example: Painter agrees to paint Owner's house a hideously ugly color desired by Owner. Instead of painting the house the agreed color, Painter uses a neutral off-white color. Although the cost of performance greatly exceeds the difference in value (painting the house the agreed color would have reduced its value), Owner is entitled to the cost of performance which is necessary to satisfy the owner's expectation.

c. **Breach by Delay in Completion.** Owner will be entitled to the **lost rental value** of the completed structure during the delay.

2. **Contractor's Damages – Breach by the Owner or Employer**. A contractor, employee, or other provider of services for a set price is normally compensated by awarding the provider one of two formulas to compensate it for the lost payment while taking into account any savings the provider may have enjoyed as a result of the breach. Either formula should yield the same result.

   a. **Contract Price Minus Expenses Saved By the Breach**. The provider is awarded the entire agreed price for the services that were to be performed, minus whatever expenses the provider has saved, in labor and materials, as a result of the recipient's repudiation or breach. This should result in the same amount as the second formula, cost incurred plus profit.

   Example: Builder agrees to construct bridge for County for $500,000. Builder expects to incur expenses of $450,000 in completing the work, resulting in a net profit of $50,000. Builder starts work and incurs $150,000 in unsalvageable expense before County repudiates. The breach by the County saved Builder $300,000. Builder can recover $200,000 based on the contract price ($500,000) minus expenses saved ($300,000) = $200,000 for its expectation recovery.

   b. **Cost Incurred Plus Profit**. In the second alternative formula the Contractor is awarded the amount it has spent in performing, up to the time of the repudiation plus whatever profit it would have earned upon completion of the job. This should result in the same total recovery as the Contract price minus expenses saved formula.

   Example: Same facts as above: Recovery based on the $150,000 cost incurred before the breach plus the $50,000 profit that would have been made on the deal ($500,000 price - $450,000 anticipated expense) yields the same $200,000 expectation recovery.

c. **Application of Formulas.** Both formulas should produce the same result.

1) **Breach Before Work Commences.** Where the Owner breaches before the Contractor has begun, the formula will result in the Contractor recovering the profit it would have earned on the job, had it been completed.

2) **Breach While Work is in Progress.** Where the Owner breaches after work has commenced, the Contractor will recover damages for the profit it would have earned, plus whatever expenses it has incurred up to the point of breach.

3) **Breach After Work is Completed or "Substantially Performed."** If the Contractor completely performs it should recover the entire contract price. If there is a delay in payment, it should recover interest on the amount due to compensate for the delay in receipt of the money.

d. **Treatment of Fixed (Overhead) and Variable Expenses**. Provider's recovery should include recovery for the portion of fixed costs attributable to the contract, but should not include amounts for anticipated variable expenses saved as a result of the breach. Fixed costs are not avoided as a result of the breach and receipt of the contract price would have offset these expenses. Variable costs, on the other hand, are avoided as a result of the breach.

Example: Contract to build new school building for a price of $10,000,000. Contractor anticipates incurring $9,500,000 in variable expenses to complete the year-long job which will be supervised full-time by Contractor's General Manager who is paid a $100,000 annual salary. Contractor's rent on its headquarters is $20,000 per year. Three months after work has begun, and $3,000,000 in materials and labor for hourly employees working on the job site has been paid, the School Board repudiates. Contractor's recovery would be $3,425,000 based on the contract price of $10,000,000, minus $6,500,000 in variable expenses saved also diminished by $75,000 (3/4 based on 9 of 12 months remaining) salary attributable to the manager who is presumably free to work on other projects. There is no deduction for the pro-rata share of the $20,000 fixed office rent.

D. CONTRACTS FOR THE SALE OF GOODS UNDER UCC ARTICLE 2

Remedies for breach of contracts for the sale of goods are governed by Article 2 of the Uniform Commercial Code.

1. **UCC Buyer's Remedies – Breach by the Seller**. Where the seller of goods is in breach, Buyer has several alternative remedies, depending on the nature of the breach.

a. **Goods Not Delivered or Defective Goods Rejected by Buyer** (or Buyer Justifiably Revokes Acceptance Due to Substantially Impairing Defect). Where the seller fails to deliver the goods or delivers nonconforming (defective) goods and the buyer either rejects or revokes acceptance due to the nonconformity, the buyer is entitled to: 1) cancel the contract; 2) recover any payment the buyer has made; and 3) recover damages based on either the cost of cover or the market value of the goods as described below.

1) **Buyer May Cancel the Contract and Refuse to Perform.** At common law this was called "rescission for breach."

2) **Buyer May Recover Any Down-Payment That Has Been Made.**

3) **Buyer May Recover Damages based On The Cost of Cover or The Market Value of Goods.**

   a) **Damages Based On The Cost Of Cover.** If the buyer purchases substitute goods, the buyer is entitled to recover damages measured by:

The Cost of Cover (a Reasonable Substitute for the Goods) - the Contract Price + Incidental Damages provided by UCC 2-715(1) + Consequential Damages provided by UCC 2-715(2) - Expenses Saved as a Result of the Breach

      i) Cover consists of the purchase of a reasonable substitute for the goods involved in the contract.

      ii) Cover must be obtained in "good faith" and "without unreasonable delay."

      iii) Buyer who fails to cover property must recover under UCC 2-713 based on the market value of the goods.

      Example: Seller failed to deliver the Vintage French Poster for the agreed price of $9,000. After extensive efforts, Buyer discovered and purchased an identical poster from another supplier for $10,000. Buyer can recover the difference between the $10,000 cost of cover and the $9,000 contract price together with the incidental expenses incurred in locating the substitute.

   b) **Damages Based on Market Value.** If the buyer is unable to cover by obtaining a substitute, or if the buyer covers in a manner inconsistent with UCC 2-712, the buyer is entitled to recover damages measured by the greater market value of the goods:

The Market Value of the Goods at the time the buyer learned of the breach; - the Contract Price + Incidental Damages provided by UCC 2-715(1) + Consequential Damages provided by UCC 2-715(2) - Expenses Saved as a Result of the Breach

Example: Buyer and Seller entered into a contract for the sale of a vintage 1969 Ford Mustang for $5,000. Seller refused to perform. At the time for delivery, the market value of the car in the city where delivery was to be made was $6,500. The buyer is entitled to the $1500 difference between the market value and contract price, together with any incidental damages suffered by the buyer in seeking an alternative or obtaining an appraisal of the vehicle, together with any foreseeable consequential damages that could not have been prevented by cover or other efforts to mitigate the loss.

i) **Repudiation**. The breach does not occur until the time for delivery of the goods. The traditional rule was that in "repudiation" cases, damages based on the market value of the goods were calculated based on the market value at the time for performance. UCC 2-713 seems to continue this by indicating that the market value is the value "at the time the buyer learned of the breach."

ii) Where repudiation occurs significantly before the time for delivery, the market might fluctuate considerably between the time of repudiation and the time delivery is due. UCC 2-610 permits an aggrieved buyer to "wait for a commercially reasonable time" after repudiation. This has led most courts to rule that the market should be measured at the time the buyer learns of the repudiation plus a commercially reasonable time.

Example: Contract for sale made in 2000 provides for delivery of 10,000 tons of coal every month for 5 years. In January 2001, Seller repudiates, refusing to perform for the remainder of the term. At common law the market value of coal would have to be measured at the time for each monthly delivery for the remaining 4 years of the contract. UCC 2-713 has been interpreted to require the use of the market value of the goods measured as of a commercially reasonable time after Buyer learns of the Seller's repudiation. A commercially reasonable time will vary, depending on market conditions, the buyer's need for the goods, and other circumstances surrounding the transaction.

iii) UCC 2-723 provides that where the action comes to trial before the time for delivery, the market is measured as of the time the buyer "learned of the repudiation."

iv) **Lack of Evidence of Market Value.** If evidence of the market value at the time and place for tender is not readily available, then use the market value within any reasonable time before or after the time the market would otherwise be measured; or the market value of a commercially reasonable alternate location may be used with any necessary adjustment for transportation costs.

b. **Damages for Breach of Warranty for Goods Accepted by Buyer under UCC 2-714.** Damages for breach of warranty are the **difference in value** between the goods as delivered and as they would have been as warranted, together with any incidental and consequential damages recoverable under UCC 2-715.

1) Where the **cost of repair** is smaller than the difference in value, the buyer will only be able to recover the cost of repair.

Example: Customer purchases a new automobile from Dealer. Because of a misadjusted engine, the auto will not start. The value of the automobile to the customer is severely diminished by the fact that it will not start. The cost of repair is $35. The Customer can recover only the cost to repair the misadjustment.

c. **Incidental Damages Under UCC 2-715(1).** In addition to damages based on the market value, cost of cover, or difference in value, a buyer may recover incidental damages.

1) **Rightfully Rejected Goods:** Incidental damages in connection with rightfully rejected goods usually consist of expenses reasonably incurred in inspecting, receiving, transporting the goods, or in their care and custody after rejection.

2) **Efforts To Obtain Cover:** Buyer's incidental damages might also include expenses of attempting to obtain cover (substitute goods)

d. **Consequential Damages Under UCC 2-715(2).** Buyer may also recover consequential damages for loss resulting from general or particular requirements and needs of which the seller had reason to know at the time of contracting and which could not have been prevented by cover or otherwise.

1) **Consequential Damages** usually consist of lost profit due to the buyer's expected use or resale of the goods.

2) **Reason To Know – Foreseeability.** Seller must have had reason to know, at the time the contract was made, of the nature of the harm that buyer would suffer as a result of the breach. "Reason to know" is the **"foreseeability"** rule of ***Hadley v. Baxendale.*** Damages are foreseeable if the breaching party knew or should have known of the potential harm at the time the contract was made.

a) **General Damages** – those which occur in the usual course of events and therefore which may reasonably be supposed to have been known.

b) **Special Damages** – harm which does not occur in the usual course of events and for which recovery is not available unless the special circumstances which gave rise to the harm were communicated to the breaching party **at the time the contract was made,** or earlier.

3) Consequential Damages are not available if the loss could have been prevented by cover, or other reasonable action by the buyer to mitigate the loss.

e. **Specific Performance for Buyer under UCC 2-716 Where Goods Are Unique or In Other Proper Circumstances.** Specific Performance is available where the remedy at law is inadequate.

1) **Unique Goods.** Specific Performance is traditionally available in contracts involving unique, one-of-a-kind goods such as precious works of art, unique antiques, heirlooms, special jewels, etc.

2) **Cover Not Available.** UCC 2-716 expands the availability of specific performance to contracts involving goods where a substitute (cover) is not readily available, or is available only with extensive or extraordinary effort, or after considerable delay, even though the goods are not unique in the traditional sense.

3) **Requirements and Output Contracts.** The Official Comments to UCC 2-716 indicate that requirements and output contracts are examples of situations where specific performance is available under the "other proper circumstances" test where market conditions may make cover difficult or impossible to obtain.

2. **UCC Seller's Remedies – Breach by the Buyer**

a. **Seller's Right To Identify Goods, Complete Manufacture, Scrap, or Stop Delivery.** When the buyer breaches or repudiates the seller may:

1) **identify goods in his possession to the contract.** Where goods are in the seller's possession or control he may identify them to the particular contract and treat them as the subject of resale;

2) **complete manufacture of any unfinished goods and identify them to the contract.** Where goods are unfinished, the seller has the option of completing their manufacture and identifying them to the contract so long as this is done in the exercise of **reasonable commercial judgment** for the purpose of **avoiding loss;**

3) **resell unfinished goods for scrap or salvage.** Alternatively, the seller may cease manufacture of the unfinished goods and resell them for their scrap or salvage value. The decision to either cease or complete manufacture must be made according to **reasonable commercial judgment for the purpose of avoiding loss**; or

4) **stop delivery.** Where goods are still in the possession of a carrier or other bailee for delivery to the buyer, the seller may stop delivery. The right to stop delivery expires after either receipt by the buyer, delivery of a negotiable document of title

for the goods to a buyer, or acknowledgment by a warehouseman (but not a carrier) of the buyer's right to possession of the goods.

b. **Resale with Damages Based On the Resale Price.** Where the buyer refuses to accept conforming goods, the seller can recover damages based on the difference between the contract price and the resale price together with any incidental damages, but less expenses saved due to the breach.

Example: Art Dealer and Homeowner enter into a contract for sale of an artistic one-of-a kind garden sculpture for a price of $20,000. Before delivery, Homeowner is transferred to another city and decides not to go ahead with the sale. A month later, and after proper notice to Homeowner, Art Dealer resells the sculpture to someone else for a price of $18,000. Dealer can recover the $2,000 difference between the contract price and the resale price from Homeowner, plus any incidental damages for storage and care of the sculpture during the month before resale.

1) **Resale Via Good Faith Commercially Reasonable Public or Private Sale.** The seller's resale may be at a pubic (auction) sale or a private sale, but must be commercially reasonable. The method, time, place, manner, and terms must all be commercially reasonable.

2) **Seller Not Accountable For Profit.** If the goods sell for greater than the resale price, together with expenses of conducting the sale, the seller is not accountable for any profit obtained from the resale.

c. **Damages Based on the Market Value.** Alternatively, the seller can recover damages based on the difference between the contract price and the market value, at the time and place for tender, plus any incidental damages, but less expenses saved because of the breach.

Example: Contract for the sale of a used car for $5,000. Buyer refuses to take delivery of the goods or pay for them. Seller does not resell the car, but instead decides to keep it. At the time Buyer was to have taken delivery and paid, the car was worth $4,500. Seller can recover the $500 difference between the $5,000 contract price and the $4,500 market value.

d. **Lost-Volume Seller Can Recover Lost Profits Under UCC 2-708(2).** Lost volume sellers who have access to additional supply and would have an additional profit if the sale had been completed. Add any incidental damages (such as storage, care, and interest expense) and subtract any value received upon a salvage sale of the goods.

1) The difference between the contract price and either the resale price under UCC 2-706 or the market value under UCC 2-708(1) is inadequate to put a "lost volume" seller in the position it would have been in had the contract been performed. Accordingly, UCC 2-708(2) permits such a seller to recover the profit it would have made on the transaction from the breaching buyer.

Example: Yacht Dealer made a contract with Boater for sale of a 30' sailboat for $50,000. Boater repudiated and two weeks later Dealer sold the same 30' yacht to a new buyer, for the same $50,000 price. If Boater had completed the sale Dealer would have been able to sell two boats, earning a profit on each transaction. Dealer is entitled to recover the profit it would have made on the sale to Boater. Dealer may also recover for incidental expenses of storing and caring for the boat for an additional two weeks.

2) Lost profit is calculated by subtracting the seller's cost of obtaining the goods (or other variable costs) from the contract price. **Profit may include reasonable overhead.**

Example: Buyer agrees to purchase sailboat for $40,000, but repudiated before taking delivery. Boat Dealer acquired sailboat for $35,000. Boat Dealer's lost profit is $5,000.

3) Lost volume seller entitled to **incidental damages** for transportation, storage, etc.

Example: In above example, Boat Dealer incurred transportation and storage charges of $350. These incidental damages may be included as part of Seller's recovery under UCC 2-708(2).

4) Language in UCC 2-708(2) regarding "credit for resale" refers to sale of otherwise worthless goods for salvage, not resale in the ordinary course.

e. **Seller's Action for the Price**. Under 2-709 the seller may recover an action for the entire agreed price where the buyer has accepted the goods or where the goods are not suitable for resale to others.

Example: Seller completes manufacture of a custom sign, containing buyer's restaurant's name, for an agreed price of $3,000. Buyer repudiates. The sign is not suitable for sale to anyone else. Seller can recover the entire $3,000 price.

Example: Seller delivers computer system to Buyer who accepts goods. Seller may recover the full contract price from Buyer.

E. CONTRACTS FOR REAL ESTATE

1. **Seller's Remedies for Buyer's Breach.** Seller can compel specific performance – an action for the full price; or obtain damages based on the difference between the contract price and the market value (Contract Price – Market Value).

2. **Buyer's Remedies for Seller's Breach.** Buyer can obtain specific performance, or recover damages based on the difference between the market value and the contract price (Market Value – Contract Price).

a. **Defects in Seller's Title.** Some jurisdictions limit the buyer to reliance damages for expenses incurred in conducting title search and preparing for performance, where seller is unable to perform due to a previously unknown defect in the seller's title.

3. **Specific Performance of Contracts for Sale of Interest in Real Estate.** Specific performance is available for breach of a contract for the sale of real estate because every parcel of real estate is considered unique. Thus, the remedy at law of money damages would be considered inadequate. Specific performance is available for the seller (vendor) or the purchaser.

F. LIMITATIONS ON RECOVERY OF DAMAGES

There are three important limits on remedies for breach of contract: Foreseeability, Mitigation, and Certainty.

1. **Foreseeability.** Damages are recoverable only if the harm for which compensation is sought was **foreseeable** by the breaching party **at the time the contract was made.**

a. Foreseeability is an **objective standard** based on what the breaching party knew or had reason to know at the time the contract was made.

1) **Reason To Know Standard of UCC 2-715.** UCC 2-715(2) regarding buyer's **consequential damages** requires that damages based on the buyer's general or particular requirements and needs are recoverable only if the seller had **reason to know** of them at the time the contract was made. The reason to know standard is the same standard as the common law foreseeability standard.

b. **General and Special Damages.** Damages are traditionally divided into two categories for purposes of determining foreseeability, **general** and **special damages.**

1) **General Damages:** for harm that occurs in the usual course of events as a **natural consequence of a breach**. Recovery of general damages is available without any special proof.

2) **Special Damages:** for harm that occurs **because of the special requirements** or needs of the innocent party or for harms that are otherwise beyond those that would ordinarily occur as a result of the breach. The plaintiff can recover for special damages only if **at the time the contract was made**, the breaching party knew that the harm would occur or the innocent party put the **breaching party on notice** of the special circumstances that would give rise to the harm if there were a breach.

Example: Boiler Manufacturer entered into contract with Laundry to sell a boiler intended for use by Laundry in its laundry and dyeing business. Manufacturer failed to provide timely delivery of the boiler causing Buyer to lose revenue generally from its inability to expand its business and also from the loss of an unusually profitable dyeing contract it made with one of its customers. Damages due to loss of revenue generally would be recoverable as a loss which occurred in the ordinary course of business, so long as it was reasonably certain. Loss of the revenue from the unusually lucrative dyeing contracts on the other hand would not be recoverable unless the Buyer notified the Manufacturer that loss of this revenue was at stake, **at the time the contract was made.**

c. **Tacit Agreement Test Rejected.** A few states still apply the more strict "tacit agreement" test, which requires more than mere notice. Under this test, liability for the harm is imposed only if "it fairly may be presumed that the breaching party would have assented to the liability if the question had been presented to him." ***Globe Refining Co. v. Landa Oil Co.***, 190 U.S. 540 (Holmes. J.). Modern courts, and UCC 2-715(2) have rejected the "tacit agreement" test in favor of the "reason to know" standard which imposes liability if the breaching party knew or should have known of the harm that would occur.

2. **Certainty.** To be recoverable the existence and amount of damages must be **reasonably certain**. It must be reasonably certain that the defendant's breach caused the harm and the amount of harm must be calculable with reasonable certainty.

a. **Speculative Lost Profits** may be difficult to prove with reasonable certainty, particularly in the case of a new business that lacks a proven track-record of producing revenue. Some courts refuse to permit proof of lost profits in the case of a new business; the modern trend is to admit the evidence. Damages due to lost profits are also uncertain in long-term requirement or output contracts for the sale of goods, or in franchise agreements, because future profits cannot be calculated that far in the future.

Example: Construction Co. promised to renovate Downtown Deli's recently rented new premises to make it suitable for use as a deli. Construction Co. never showed up to do the work resulting in a two month delay in Deli's opening. Deli will be unable to recover the profits it would have made during those two months, because it cannot prove the amount of business the new restaurant would have done during these first two months.

b. **Reliance Damages As an Alternative.** Damages based on the innocent party's reasonably foreseeable reliance expense are used as an alternative to expectation damages where the value of the lost expectation is too uncertain or speculative.

1) Reliance damages may not, however, exceed the value of the innocent party's expectation. The innocent party may not shift the loss it would have suffered as a result of the contract to the breaching party simply because of the breach.

Example: Promoter enters into contract with Rock and Roll Band to perform at concert. Promoter incurs $100,000 expense in securing an Arena for the performance, advertising the show, and preparing tickets to be sold. After these expenses have been incurred, the Band reneges because it has found a better deal in another nearby city for the same date. Ticket sales for the concert in the nearby city are so poor, however, that they would have only earned Promoter $60,000. Promoter is unable to recover its lost expectation due to uncertainty about revenue from the concert. Normally Promoter would be able to recover the $100,000 spent in reliance on the Band's appearance, as an expense incurred in foreseeable reliance on the contract. In this case, the Band will have the opportunity to show that ticket sales would be so poor that Promoter would not have recouped the $100,000 even if the Band had performed.

c. **No Recovery for Mental Distress.** Damages for mental distress or anguish are not recoverable for breach of contract absent circumstances that are likely to cause mental distress in the event of a breach.

Example: Employee for a specific term is fired, without cause, in breach of his employment contract. Employee cannot recover damages for mental distress or anguish.

Example: Funeral Home enters into contract to display body of Customer's deceased mother at funeral service and breaches by displaying the wrong body. Damages for mental distress are available because of the emotional suffering inherently involved in the contract.

3. **Avoidability – Mitigation**. The non-breaching party has a **duty to mitigate its damages.** The non-breaching party cannot recover for losses that it could have mitigated or avoided by its own reasonable actions, after breach, to prevent the harm.

a. **Mitigation in General**

1) Innocent party may not recover for expenses, incurred after the breach that could **reasonably have been avoided**, e.g., a builder in a construction contract must cease work upon learning of the owner's breach.

2) Innocent party must take **positive reasonable steps to limit the harm** that will be caused by the breach, e.g., an aggrieved employee must seek employment of a substantially similar character; an aggrieved seller must conduct a commercially reasonable resale of goods the buyer has wrongfully rejected; the buyer must make reasonable effort to obtain cover or be barred from consequential damages that could have been prevented.

b. **Mitigation in Contracts for the Sale of Goods under UCC Article 2**

1) **Buyer's Duty To Mitigate Where Seller Is In Breach Through Cover or Otherwise**.

a) **Buyer may cover** under UCC 2-706 by purchasing a reasonable substitute in good faith and without unreasonable delay and recover the difference between the cost of cover and the contract price. If the buyer does not cover, damages will be measured by the difference between the market value (at the time the buyer learned of the breach) and the contract price.

b) Consequential Damages under UCC 2-715(2) are **not recoverable** if the consequential harm could have been prevented by obtaining substitute goods (cover) or by other action taken to mitigate damages.

2) **Seller's Duty To Mitigate When Buyer Is In Breach.** The seller's duty to mitigate is most often accomplished via commercially reasonable **resale**.

a) Seller may stop delivery of any goods in transit.

b) **Unfinished Goods.** Seller has the right, under UCC 2-704, to exercise **reasonable commercial judgment**, for the purposes of avoiding loss, to either complete or cease manufacture of goods which are unfinished. This permits the seller to exercise its reasonable commercial judgment to either finish the goods and wholly identify them to the contract or to resell the partially completed items for scrap or salvage.

c) Resale must be conducted in a **commercially reasonable manner** with notice to the buyer of the time and place of any public sale (auction) or the time after which the goods will be resold in any private sale. If resale is for an amount greater than the contract price, seller is not required to pay the profit to the breaching buyer.

c. **Employment Contracts.** Each party is required to use reasonable efforts to obtain a substitute.

1) **Employer in Breach.** Employee must use reasonable efforts to obtain **substantially similar employment** although it may not be for the same rate of pay. If the employee is offered substantially similar employment and turns it down, the employee's damages will be reduced by the amount the employee would have earned had the proffered employment been accepted. Wages earned by the employee in a different job will be deducted from the employee's recovery, even if the job is of a different kind or quality, even though the employee would have been justified in turning down the alternative employment because of its inferior kind or different rank. However, if the job is one that employee could have completed while still working for the breaching employer, the wages will not be deducted from her recovery.

Example: Professional Chauffeur is fired, in breach of employment contract, from his job as a stretch-limousine driver. The next week the Chauffeur turns down an offer of employment as a school bus driver. The amount the Chauffeur would have earned driving the school bus will not be deducted from his recovery from his previous employer because driving a school bus is work of a different kind and quality than driving a limousine.

Example: The same as above, except that the Chauffeur accepts the job driving the school bus, but at a lower rate of pay. The wages earned driving the bus will be deducted from his recovery, unless he could have performed both jobs, one in the day and the other at night.

Example: The same as the first example above, except that the Chauffeur failed to respond to ads in the local newspaper seeking experienced limousine drivers and the Chauffeur was the most qualified person for those jobs. The wages the Chauffeur would have earned will most likely be deducted from his recovery if his former Employer can prove that he likely would have been hired for the advertised jobs.

2) **Employee in Breach.** Employer must use reasonable efforts to engage similarly qualified worker or be barred from recovery of consequential damages.

d. **Construction Contracts.** Builder may not continue performance of construction contract after learning of Owner's repudiation and recover for expenses incurred in completing construction.

Example: Painter and Homeowner enter into contract for painting of Homeowner's residence for a price of $5,000. After Painter completes 25% of the job, incurring $1,000 in expenses for labor and materials, Homeowner repudiates, ordering Painter to quit. Painter ignores Homeowner and completes the job, incurring an additional $3,000 in costs. Painter will recover the contract price of $5,000 minus the $3,000 in expenses the Painter could have saved if he has ceased work when Homeowner repudiated.

G. LIMITED REMEDIES, LIQUIDATED DAMAGES AND PENALTIES

1. **Limited Remedy Provisions in Contracts For Sale of Goods Under UCC 2-719.** Limited remedy provisions, such as those ordinarily found in contracts for the sale of goods or express manufacturer's warranties, frequently limit a buyer to repair or replacement of the defective goods and exclude recovery for consequential damages caused by any breach of the warranty.

a. **Optional Unless Made Exclusive.** Use of a remedy provision in the contract is "optional" unless the Remedy provision is expressly agreed to be exclusive; if exclusive, it is the sole remedy.

b. **Failure of Limited Remedy's Essential Purpose.** Under UCC 2-719, a limited remedy is unenforceable where circumstances cause it to "fail of its essential purpose."

1) **Other Remedies Available.** If the limited remedy fails of its essential purpose, the other remedies provided by the UCC, such as money damages or specific performance, are available. A limited remedy provision fails of its essential purpose when circumstances prevent it from providing the innocent party with the remedy contemplated by the contract.

2) **Repair or Replacement.** A buyer may resort to other remedies provided in the UCC when the limited remedy of "repair" or "replacement" does not provide the buyer of goods with goods which conform to the warranties provided under the contract, such as where repairs are ineffective or replacement goods contain the same defects as the original.

   Example: New Auto purchased under contract providing for "repair" as the exclusive remedy for any defects. The brakes failed and Seller made several efforts to effectuate repairs but could not correct the problem. The limited remedy of "repair" has failed of its essential purpose. As a result, Buyer may resort to other remedies provided in the UCC, including "revocation of acceptance" due to "substantially impairing defect" and the recovery of damages based on the cost of cover, etc.

3) **New Auto Lemon Laws**. New automobile "lemon laws" typically permit a seller of a new automobile to have a specified number of chances to correct a defect. If the defect cannot be repaired after these specified attempts, the buyer is entitled to a refund.

c. **Unconscionability of Limited Remedies.** A limited remedy in a contract for the sale of goods, that prevents the recovery of consequential damages **for personal injury in connection with consumer goods** is "prima facie" unconscionable — presumed to be unconscionable. However, a limited remedy that prevents recovery of consequential damages, where the loss is "commercial," is not presumed unconscionable. UCC 2-719(3).

   Example: A provision in contract for sale of automobile to Homeowner limited the buyer's remedy for any defects in the materials or workmanship to repair or replacement. It disclaimed liability for any consequential damages occurring as a result of any breach of warranty concerning the goods. This provision is presumed unconscionable as applied to Homeowner's action to recover for spinal injuries he suffered as a result of defective brakes.

2. **Liquidated Damage Provisions (Penalties).** Contracts frequently contain "liquidated damage" provisions, setting an amount of damages or a formula for calculation of damages. The enforceability of liquidated damage clauses depends on: 1) whether the agreed amount is **reasonable compared to the anticipated or actual damages** caused by the breach; and 2) the **difficulty of calculating the actual damages**.

a. **Reasonable Compared To Actual or Anticipated Harm.** Liquidated damages are **not** reasonable compared to the anticipated damages where the amount is a fixed sum that does not take into account the range of potential harm from varying degrees of breach. To be enforceable the agreed amount must be tailored to the harm caused by the breach.

Example: One-year employment contract contains a provision providing for $1,000 agreed damages for any breach by the Employee. The term is unenforceable because it is a flat sum that does not take into account whether the breach occurs early in the year or late in the year.

b. **Anticipated Difficulty of Calculating Actual Damages.** Where actual damages are easily calculated, an agreed remedy that is disproportionate to the actual harm will probably not be enforced, even though it was reasonable compared to the anticipated harm. This is particularly true where circumstances demonstrate that the innocent party would suffer no harm from the breach.

H. RESTITUTION

Restitution is a broad remedy, used in a variety of circumstances beyond its use as a remedy for breach of contract. It is used in three distinct situations in a contracts setting: as a basic remedy for breach of contract; as a remedy for a breaching party who has partially performed; and to provide a remedy where the parties have performed and a contract is found to be unenforceable.

1. **Rescission and Restitution for Material Breach of Contract**

a. Rescission for material breach, with restitution of benefits conferred before the breach is a traditional remedy for breach of contract. Recovery in restitution may be permitted to exceed the value of the innocent party's lost expectation.

b. Rescission and restitution are not available in favor of a party who has substantially performed where the only performance remaining due by the party in breach is payment of the price. Recovery is limited to the contract price for the performance rendered.

c. In contracts for the sale of goods, UCC 2-711 permits the buyer to recover any part of the purchase price that has been paid, if the seller repudiates, fails to deliver, or where the buyer rightfully rejects or rightfully revokes acceptance of goods the seller has delivered.

Example: Buyer contracts with Seller to pay $7,000 for automobile with fair market value of only $6,500, and makes a $500 down payment. Seller repudiates prior to delivery. Buyer can recover his entire $500 down payment in restitution even though Buyer would have suffered a $500 loss had the contract been performed by paying $7,000 for a car worth only $6,500.

2. **Restitution In Favor of The Breaching Party**. A party in breach is entitled to recover in quasi-contract for the value of the benefit of his part performance, up to the time of his breach, to prevent unjust enrichment.

   Example: Builder begins work under a contract for the construction of an antenna tower for a Radio Station, completing 2/3 of the work before repudiating the contract. Builder may recover for the value of the benefit conferred, despite his breach.

   a. Recovery in restitution will be offset by the loss caused to the innocent party.

   b. Some courts refuse to award restitution to a breaching party in cases involving an intentional or malicious breach.

3. **Restitution In Absence of Contract or When Agreement Is not Enforceable.** Recovery is available in ***quasi-contract, or contract implied in law,*** where there is no agreement but relief is necessary to prevent unjust enrichment. Quasi-contract can be used where there is no agreement between the parties and where a **benefit has been conferred** under circumstances where there is a **reasonable expectation of compensation** and the person who conferred a benefit was **not acting as a volunteer**.

   a. **Restitution for Benefit Conferred Under Circumstances Where Compensation Reasonably Expected**. Restitution is available on a theory of **contract implied in law** where a benefit is conferred on a person under circumstances which indicate that the conferral of the benefit was not a gift and that payment was expected.

      1) **Voluntary Receipt of Benefit under Circumstances Indicating Payment Was Expected.** A person who consciously receives a benefit conferred under circumstances which indicate that payment for the benefit was expected may not retain the benefit without compensation.

      2) **Involuntary Conferral of Benefit.** Absent an emergency, a person has no obligation to pay for a benefit which was not sought nor consciously received.

         Example: Without prior invitation, Lawn Mowing Crew shows up at Owner's house while he is away and mows his extensive lawn. Owner has no obligation to pay for the benefit conferred.

      3) **Restitution for Emergency Services.** Restitution is owed for emergency services conferred on a person who was unable to express assent to the conferral of the benefit because of her injuries or other circumstances.

         Example: Victim arrives unconscious at the Hospital where Doctors provide emergency medical treatment in an effort to save Victim. Despite their efforts, Victim dies. Doctors and the Hospital have a claim in quasi-contract for the reasonable value of their services, which conferred a benefit on the Victim despite his failure to survive.

4) **Benefit Intended As a Gift.** Where the benefit was intended as a gift, or where the benefit was conferred by someone acting as a volunteer without expectation of payment, restitution is not available. Where the parties are in a close personal relationship to one-another, there is a presumption that the benefits were conferred as a gift and not with the reasonable expectation of payment.

b. **Performance under Unenforceable Agreement.** Restitution is available where there has been part-performance by one party under an agreement which is unenforceable under the statute of frauds, due to mistake, impossibility, or frustration of purpose, or due to lack of contractual capacity of the parties.

Example: Employee works for 9 months under the terms of an oral employment contract for a term of 2 years. Because the oral contract cannot be performed within a year of its making, it is unenforceable under the statute of frauds. The Employee is entitled to recover in quasi-contract for the value of his performance during the 9 months partial performance in order to prevent unjust enrichment of the Employer.

Watch Out!

Always look for a valid contract first. If there is one, quasi-contract cannot apply. But if there is no valid contract, a quasi-contract will provide a remedy if the plaintiff has suffered a loss or rendered services.

I. EQUITABLE REMEDIES: SPECIFIC PERFORMANCE AND INJUNCTIONS

Equitable remedies are available where the remedy at law is inadequate and the balance of equities favors relief.

1. **Types of Equitable Remedies**

a. **Specific Performance.** Specific performance orders the defendant to perform the contract according to its terms. Failure to perform as ordered is punishable by contempt of court.

b. **Injunctions.** An injunction prohibits the defendant from engaging in some sort of conduct.

1) Where the risk of irreparable harm can be shown, the court may impose a short-term **Temporary Restraining Order** on little or no advance notice, to prevent the defendant from engaging in conduct that would be hard to reverse and to thus preserve the status quo until the court can conduct a hearing on a preliminary injunction.

2) A **Preliminary Injunction** is available, pending a full trial, where the plaintiff can show the likelihood of ultimate success on the merits and that irreparable harm will occur in the absence of an injunction pending trial.

3) A **Permanent Injunction** is granted where the plaintiff prevails on the merits, the remedy at law of money damages is inadequate, and the balance of equities favors the requested injunction.

c. **Constructive Trusts.** A constructive trust declares that the defendant's ownership of property is **in trust** for the benefit of the plaintiff, and thus imposes a fiduciary duty on the defendant to act as trustee for the plaintiff.

2. **Adequacy of the Legal Remedy**. Equitable remedies are available only where the remedy at law of money damages is inadequate. Money damages are inadequate where there is no substitute for the promised performance; or where recovery of money damages is unlikely due to the limited resources of the defendant.

3. **Balancing of Equities.** Equitable remedies are available only where a balancing of the equities favors relief. The court **will measure the harm to the plaintiff** if relief is not granted with the **burden imposed on the defendant** if the court orders specific performance or an injunction and determine if relief is warranted.

4. **Equitable Remedies In Specific Types of Contracts**

a. **Real Estate**. All real estate is considered unique. Therefore, the legal remedy of money damages is inadequate and specific performance is usually available for breach of a contract for the sale of an interest in real estate. Specific performance is available to the seller or the buyer.

b. **Goods – Personal Property**

1) **For the Buyer**. The traditional rule is that specific performance is available only when the goods are unique. UCC 2-716 provides specific performance **when the goods are unique or in light of other proper circumstances,** including the unavailability or difficulty of obtaining cover. This includes goods that are not unique in the traditional sense of "one-of-a-kind" but where, due to market conditions or otherwise, obtaining a substitute is impossible or difficult. Specific Performance is available in requirements and output contracts.

2) **For the Seller.** The seller can obtain specific performance, in the form of payment of the price, where the goods are specially manufactured for the buyer and unsuitable for sale to others, or where they have been accepted by the buyer. If the seller is awarded the price, the buyer is entitled to the goods or the proceeds of the sale thereof.

c. **Services – Employment, Contracts to Build or Repair, and Other Personal Services**

1) **Specific Performance Unavailable.** Specific performance is unavailable in contracts for services, even when the services are unique or obtaining a substitute is difficult, because of the harshness of ordering someone to perform or accept services from another when one of the parties no longer wishes to perform, but also because of the **difficulty of supervision**. Compelling the performance of services may also violate the **Constitution's 13th amendment which prohibits involuntary servitude**.

2) **Injunctions.** An injunction may be available where the contract contains an express or implied **negative covenant**. This may be true in personal service contracts where the defendant would not be able to work for the plaintiff and a third party at the same time.

Example: Athlete agreed to play football for the Dallas Cowboys, a professional football team. While still under contract with the Cowboys he breached and entered into another contract to play for a team in a competing football league. The Dallas Cowboys could not obtain an order compelling him to specifically perform, because of the 13th amendment and the difficulty of supervision. However, the Cowboys were able to obtain an injunction against his playing for a team in the competing league. Performance of his contract with the Cowboys was incompatible with playing for another team, which would justify the court in concluding that there was an implied negative covenant not to play football for anyone else.

a) Covenants not to compete are enforceable, by an injunction, so long as the covenant is reasonable in scope and duration.

5. **Mutuality.** Equitable remedies are sometimes said to be subject to a requirement of **mutuality.** Mutuality requires that the defendant be able to obtain an equitable remedy, if the plaintiff were in breach, before the plaintiff can obtain an equitable remedy from the defendant.

Example: Defendant agreed to provide Plaintiff with a place to live during the Plaintiff's life, and to transfer his home to the Plaintiff upon the Defendant's death, in exchange for Plaintiff's agreement to provide nursing and household care services to the Defendant during the Defendant's life. The Plaintiff will be unable to obtain specific performance of the promise to provide housing and a transfer of the Defendant's house, because specific performance would not be available to the Defendant if the Plaintiff were to breach.

6. **Defenses To Equitable Remedies.** Equity provides supplemental defenses, in addition to the standard defenses to a claim for breach of contract, that the defendant can use to resist an equitable remedy:

a. **unclean hands:** wrongdoing or inequitable conduct by the party seeking equitable relief.

b. **laches:** prejudicial delay in bringing the claim. This is different from the statute of limitations.

c. **sale to a BFP:** transfer of the property that is the subject of the dispute to a bona fide purchaser for value, making specific performance impossible.

J. ELECTION OF REMEDIES

The traditional doctrine of election of remedies prevents a plaintiff from combining a recovery of expectation damages for breach of contract and restitution. The plaintiff must choose between **rescinding the contract** and recovering in **restitution** *or* **enforcing the contract** and recovering **damages for breach**, usually measured by the value of the plaintiff's lost expectations. It sometimes also operates to prevent a plaintiff from altering the remedy it is seeking, during the pendency of a lawsuit, where the other party has materially changed its position in reliance on the original remedy sought.

1. **Election Between Rescission and Enforcement.** At common law a plaintiff was said to have the option of suing to enforce the contract, by seeking damages for the value it lost due to the breach or by seeking specific performance of the contract, or to seek to rescind the contract, return any benefits received from the breaching party, and seek to recover any benefits conferred on the party in breach in restitution. Thus, the election of remedies was between rescission and restitution *or* enforcement of the contract.

2. **Rejection of Doctrine of Election of Remedies.** The Restatement of Contracts 2d, § 378 and Article 2 of the UCC reject the traditional doctrine of election of remedies. Both permit a plaintiff to combine theories of recovery so long as the combination does not result in over-compensating the plaintiff.

3. **Change of Position in Reliance on Remedy.** Where the breaching party materially changes its position in reliance on a plaintiff's pursuit of a particular remedy, the plaintiff will not be permitted to amend its complaint to seek an alternate remedy that would impair the breaching party's change of position.

   Example: Seller repudiates contract for sale of real estate. The aggrieved Buyer brings an action seeking money damages based on the difference in value between the contract price and the market value of the land. In reliance on the Buyer's apparent decision not to seek specific performance, the Seller, who still owns the land, makes substantial improvements to the land. The Buyer is thereafter prevented from amending its complaint to seek specific performance instead of money damages.

X. THIRD PARTY RIGHTS: THIRD PARTY BENEFICIARIES AND ASSIGNMENTS

Persons who were not parties to the original contract can have rights under the contract in two situations: 1) where the person was an "intended" third-party beneficiary of the contract; or 2) where the person has received an assignment of rights under the contract. A person who is not a party to the original contract may also have duties under the contract where duties have been delegated to a third party who has promised to perform those duties.

Watch Out!

Almost any contract is assignable. However, notable exceptions include:

- Assignments that would substantially change the obligor's duty or risk, such as personal service contracts involving unique services.
- Assignments of future rights to arise from future contracts (not to be confused with future rights in contracts that are already in existence).
- Assignments prohibited by law.

A. THIRD PARTY BENEFICIARIES

At one time, persons not a party to a contract had no rights under the contract due to a lack of "privity." Modern contract law extends rights under a contract to intended beneficiaries, but deprives incidental beneficiaries of the right to enforce the contract or recover damages for breach.

1. **Intended Beneficiaries**. Intended beneficiaries are persons, not parties to the original contract, who have the right to enforce a contract by recovering damages, or otherwise. A person is an intended beneficiary if the promisee, the person to whom the promise in question was made, entered into the contract for the purpose of providing a benefit to the third party. Traditionally third parties had rights to enforce a contract only if they were creditor or donee beneficiaries. Modern rules permit any person who was intended by the promisee to have rights to enforce the contract as an intended beneficiary.

   a. **Creditor Beneficiaries**. A traditional circumstance indicating that a third party is an intended beneficiary occurs where the promisee owes or believes he owes a legal duty to the beneficiary that will be discharged by the performance of the promisor. When performance of the contract made directly to the third party will discharge the promisee's duty to the third party, the third party is an intended beneficiary with rights under the contract. The third party is a creditor of the promisee.

   Example: Harry owed $300 to Loretta. Later, Fred purchased goods from Harry and promised to make payment by paying Harry's debt to Loretta. Loretta is a third-party beneficiary of Fred's promise to Harry. Loretta was a creditor of Harry, the promisee. Fred made a promise to Harry that he would render a performance directly to the third party, Loretta. A principal purpose of Harry, the promisee, was to benefit his creditor Loretta by satisfying his debt to her.

1) **Delegation of Duty Creates Third-party Beneficiary Contract.** When a party to a contract delegates his contractual duties to another who agrees to perform them, the promise of the person who will perform the duties creates third-party, creditor beneficiary rights in the original obligee.

   Example: Homeowner owes $80,000 to Lender. Homeowner sells his house to Buyer who "assumes" the $80,000 mortgage debt, promising to pay the $80,000 owed to Lender by Homeowner. Homeowner has delegated his duty to pay the $80,000 to Buyer. Buyer's promise to Homeowner to pay $80,000 to Lender gives Lender the right, as a third-party beneficiary of Buyer's promise, to recover the $80,000 from Buyer.

b. **Donee Beneficiaries**. A donee beneficiary traditionally had rights under a contract. A third person is a donee beneficiary when performance does not discharge a debt to the third party but, instead, effectuates a gift to the third party. Where the promisee enters into the contract with the purpose of conferring a gift on the third party, the third party was traditionally called a "donee" beneficiary who had rights under the contract.

   Example: Son enters into contract with Gardener, promising to pay Gardener for mowing lawn at his Mother's house. Mother is a third-party intended donee beneficiary of Gardener's promise, made to Son, that Gardener will mow Mother's lawn. Mother is not a creditor beneficiary because Son has no legal obligation to mow Mother's lawn. The intent of the promisee, Son, was to confer a benefit to Mother.

c. **Circumstances Indicating Intent To Benefit a Third Party.** The Restatement 2d of Contracts no longer uses the terms creditor and donee beneficiary as categories of "intended" beneficiaries. Some courts, however, use the categories where they apply. Modern law extends rights to any third-party, where a principal purpose of the promisee in making the agreement was to benefit the third party. A variety of factors are used to determine if the promisee intended the third-party to have rights under the contract. These include:

   1) performance will be **rendered directly to third-party;**

   2) performance will **discharge a legal duty of the promisee to the third-party;**

   3) **the Contract names the third-party** who will be benefited by the contract;

   4) existence of a **relationship between the promisee and third-party** that would make it reasonable to infer an intent by the promisee to benefit the third party.

2. **Incidental Beneficiaries.** Incidental beneficiaries do not have rights under the contract. Incidental beneficiaries are persons who will only incidentally benefit from performance under the contract. A person is an incidental beneficiary, with no rights to enforce the contract, if the promisee did not enter into the contract for the purpose of conferring rights or a benefit on the third-party.

3. **Third-Party Beneficiary Rights in Specific Types of Contracts**

   a. **Construction Contracts.** In typical construction settings, a vertical agreement between sub-contractor and general contractor does not confer third-party beneficiary rights on the owner to recover from the sub-contractor directly. Likewise, the traditional rule prevents one contractor on the project from recovering horizontally against another contractor on the same job.

   Example: Owner enters into separate contracts with Electrician and Plumber in connection with construction of a house. Plumber enters into sub-contract with Supplier to provide goods necessary for plumbing work. Owner is not an intended third-party beneficiary of contract between Plumber and Supplier and has no right to sue Supplier for failure to deliver necessary items. Likewise, Electrician is not an intended third-party beneficiary of contract between Owner and Plumber.

   b. **Extension of Warranty Rights in Contracts for Sale of Goods**. UCC 2-318 provides three alternate rules for extending warranty protection in contracts for sale of goods. All three alternatives extend protection, beyond the buyer, to third parties who may suffer injury as a result of a breach of warranty in connection with the goods. The buyer is always protected; UCC 2-318 specifies which third-parties, other than the buyer, will enjoy protection.

      1) Alternative A extends protection to any **natural person who is a member of the buyer's family or household or guest of the buyer in his home if it is reasonable to expect that person to use, consume or be affected by the goods** and who suffers **personal injury** as a result of the breach of warranty. This alternative does not extend warranty protection to passerbys even though they might reasonably be expected to use or be affected by the goods.

      2) Alternative B extends protection to **any natural person who it is reasonable to expect to use, consume, or be affected by the goods** who suffers **personal injury**. This alternative extends protection to any person personally injured so long as that person might reasonably have been expected to use or be affected by the goods.

      Example: Law School purchases bottled beverages for reception to be conducted at Law School. During reception, soda bottle explodes, injuring an Alumnus of the law school who was standing next to the bottle when the explosion occurred. Under alternative B the Alumnus has rights as a third-party beneficiary because the Alum was a person who it was reasonable to expect to be affected by the goods who suffered personal injury. Under alternative A, the Alum would not be able to recover because Alum is not a guest in the household of the Law School.

3) Alternative C extends protection to **any person,** whether an individual, partnership, or corporation, who may **reasonably be expected to use, consume or be affected by the warranty** and who is **injured in any way** by the breach of warranty. This alternative extends protection beyond natural persons to businesses and other entities, and extends protection for property damage or economic loss as a result of a breach of warranty. The principal limitation is that the injured person must have been reasonably expected to use, consume or be affected by the warranty.

c. **Payment Bonds**. General contractors are frequently required, by the terms of their contracts with the owner of the project, to furnish a bond to ensure payment by the contractor for all debts owed by the contractor to suppliers and sub-contractors who contribute to the project. Suppliers, sub-contractors, and laborers are permitted to recover as intended third-party beneficiaries of the bond.

d. **Public Works Contracts**. Private citizens sometimes assert rights as third-party beneficiaries of certain types of government contracts, such as those between a private water company and the city to supply water to city fire hydrants, or between highway construction firms and state government. Private citizens have not been treated as intended beneficiaries where liability for personal injury or other consequential damages was at stake, such as where a building burned for lack of water to the fire hydrants or where an accident occurred on a highway because of faulty construction. However, private citizens have been permitted to enforce contracts that have established rate structures on utility companies.

4. **Vesting of Rights of Intended Beneficiaries – Modification of Third-Party Beneficiary Contracts.** The original parties to the contract cannot alter the rights of the third party after those rights have **vested.** The rights of a third-party beneficiary vest when the third-party:

   a. **manifests assent to the contract** in a manner invited or sought by the parties;

   b. **reasonably relies on the contract** by altering his position in some material way; or

   c. **initiates suit to enforce the contract.** A court action to enforce the contract cannot be avoided by the promisor persuading the promisee to agree to a modification or discharge of the third party beneficiary contract.

5. **Defenses under Third-Party Beneficiary Contracts.** In an action brought by a third-party beneficiary to enforce a contract made for that party's benefit, the promisor may assert defenses he has under his contract with the promisee and, in some circumstances, may assert defenses the promisee holds based on any agreement between the promisee and the third-party beneficiary.

a. **Promisor's Defenses**. The promisor may always assert defenses it has arising out of the contract between the promisor and the promisee. If the promisor has the right to withhold or terminate performance because of some material breach by the promisee, the promisor can assert that defense in an action brought by the third-party beneficiary.

Example: Owner fraudulently induces Buyer to purchase home with Buyer promising to pay Owner's $60,000 outstanding mortgage debt to Bank as part of the price of the home. Buyer's fraud defense against Owner can be asserted in an action brought by Bank to recover $60,000 debt. Bank, however, will retain ability to enforce mortgage, enforcing Owner's original promise to pay.

b. **Promisee's Defenses**. Whether the promisor may assert the promisee's defenses depends on the nature of the promise made by the promisor. If the promisor promised to perform "the promisee's duties" the promisor will be able to assert defenses available to the promisee. If, instead, the promisor made an absolute promise to render a specific performance to the third-party beneficiary, without reference to the duties of the promisee, then the promisee's defenses cannot be asserted by the promisor. In any event, the promisor will be able only to assert defenses of the promisee which arise out of the transaction which the promisor has agreed to perform and not claims or defenses arising from collateral transactions between the promisee and the third-party beneficiary.

Example: Buyer purchases Greenacre from Owner, promising Owner he will pay "Owner's Mortgage Debt" to Bank. Buyer will be able to assert any defense Owner could have asserted against the Bank because Buyer promised only to pay whatever debt Owner owed to Bank.

Example: Buyer purchases Blackacre from Owner, promising Owner he will pay $70,000 to Bank. Buyer will not be able to assert defenses Owner may have against Bank as Buyer made an absolute promise to pay $70,000 to the Bank.

6. **Right of Promisee To Sue Promisor**. Most jurisdictions now deviate from the traditional rule and permit the promisee to maintain an action against the promisor for breach of contract.

a. In cases involving a **donee beneficiary**, the promisee will usually have no actual damages, but may be able to obtain specific performance, or an injunction, using the lack of damages to the promisee as establishing the inadequacy of the legal remedy. This is particularly true where unjust enrichment of the promisor would otherwise occur.

b. If the third-party is a **creditor beneficiary**, the promisee will suffer actual damages as a result of any breach by the promisor who will have failed to satisfy the promisee's duties to the third-party beneficiary. Where the breach has made it necessary for the promisee to perform its original obligations, the promisee can recover damages on account of the breach. Where the promisee has not yet performed, the promisee can compel specific performance.

7. **Effect of Third Party Beneficiary Contract On Ability of Third-Party to Recover From Promisee.** A third party beneficiary contract will have no effect on any liability of the promisee to the third party, unless there is a novation.

   a. **Creditor Beneficiary Can Recover From Promisor or Promisee, But Not Both.** Existence of third-party beneficiary contract will not usually discharge promisee's liability to a creditor third-party beneficiary. Where the promisee owes an obligation to the third-party beneficiary, the third-party can join the promisee on its original debt and the promisor on its obligation to pay the promisee's debt, but may obtain only a **single recovery.**

      Example: Holly owes $1,000 to Lawrence. Holly sells his car to Fox for $1,000 with Fox promising to pay Holly's debt to Lawrence, making Lawrence a third-party creditor beneficiary of Fox's promise to Holly. Lawrence can sue Holly on the original $1,000 debt or sue Fox on Fox's promise to Holly. Lawrence, however, cannot recover more than a total of $1,000.

   b. **Novation Discharges Promisee.** If the creditor beneficiary accepts a **novation**, substituting the liability of the promisor for that of the promisee, the promisor's liability is discharged. This can occur only via agreement of the third-party to accept the promisor's performance as a complete substitute for the liability of the promisee.

      Example: Holly owes $1,000 to Lawrence. Holly sells his car to Fox for $1,000 with Fox promising to pay Holly's debt to Lawrence and Lawrence agreeing to accept Fox's promise as a complete substitute for Holly's obligation, discharging Holly's liability. There has been a novation and Lawrence can recover only from Fox.

   c. A **donee beneficiary** has no right to sue the promisee even if the beneficiary has relied on the making of the promise. A donee beneficiary's rights are limited to those against the promisor.

      Example: In exchange for plumbing services at Lawyer's home, Lawyer promises to provide legal services to Plumber's Brother. Lawyer fails to perform the promised services for the Brother. Brother, as a third-party donee beneficiary, has rights against the Lawyer, but has no right of recourse against the Plumber.

Watch Out!

Remember that the third party beneficiary's rights cannot vest until he or she becomes aware of the contract. Therefore, before a third party beneficiary learns of the existence of a contract, it can be modified or rescinded, without regard for the rights of that beneficiary.

B. ASSIGNMENT AND DELEGATION

Persons who were not parties to the original contract can also acquire rights and responsibilities under the contract by assignment of contractual rights or delegation of contractual duties.

1. Assignment of Rights and Delegation of Duties Distinguished

a. **Assignment of Rights.** An assignment of rights occurs when a person to whom a performance is owed (the assignor) transfers the right to receive that performance to another person (the assignee). The person who owes the performance (the obligor) must render the assigned duty to the assignee. The right assigned is frequently, though not always, a right to receive payment, requiring the obligor to pay a debt, originally owed to the assignor, to the assignee. In a simple assignment of rights, the assignee has assumed no duty to render any performance to the obligor.

Example: D borrows money from Y promising to repay it. Y transfers the right to receive D's payment to X. D is the Obligor. Y is the original Obligee and Assignor. X is the Assignee.

D -----------------------> Y ---------------------------> X
Obligor Assignor Assignee

b. **Delegation of Duties.** A delegation of duties occurs when a person who owes a duty (the obligor) transfers the duty to render performance to a third person (the delagatee). The person to whom performance is owed (the obligee) has a right to recover from the delagatee who has assumed the duty to perform.

1) **Delegation May Include Assignment of Rights.** When a duty to render a performance is delegated it may or may not be accompanied by an assignment of the right to be paid for the performance of the duty.

2) **Third-Party Beneficiary Contract Involved in Delegation.** A delegation of duties always involves a third-party beneficiary contract with the obligee as a third-party creditor beneficiary of the contract of delegation.

Example: Painter Phil enters into a contract to paint Owner's home. Unable to perform himself, Phil enters into a contract with Larry, delegating to Larry the duty to paint Owner's home. Phil is the obligor and delagator. Larry is the delagatee. Owner is the obligee and is a creditor third party beneficiary of the agreement between Larry and Phil. Phil may assign to Larry the right to receive payment from Owner; or Phil might just pay Larry and collect from Owner on his own.

2. **Assignment of Rights**. An assignment is the transfer of a right to performance of a duty owed under a contract from an assignor, to an assignee.

a. **Form of Assignment.** For an assignment to be effective the assignor must manifest his intent to transfer the right either to the assignee or to a third person. It need not be communicated to the obligor.

1) **Statute of Frauds for Assignment of Accounts or Chattel Paper under UCC Article 9.** Where the right assigned is an account or chattel paper, the requirements of UCC Article 9 must be satisfied. The transaction is treated as a **security interest**, except that the debtor is not liable for a deficiency and not entitled to any surplus upon collection of the accounts or chattel paper.

a) **Written Security Agreement Required.** For the assignment or "security interest" to be effective there must be a written agreement containing description of the accounts or chattel paper and signature of assignor (debtor).

i) **Signature.** A signature is any symbol used or adopted with the intent to authenticate. It may consist of a handwritten name, a rubber stamp, or even use of letterhead stationary if the paper containing the mark was adopted with the intent to authenticate the writing.

ii) **Description of Collateral.** The writing must **reasonably identify** the accounts and chattel paper which are the subject of the assignment.

iii) **Possession of Chattel Paper in Lieu of Signed Writing.** Where the assignee is in possession of the chattel paper, pursuant to an oral agreement, no writing is necessary.

b) **Assignor Must Have Rights in The Collateral.** For the assignment to be effective the assignor (or **debtor**) must have rights in the accounts or chattel paper involved.

c) **Value Given by the Secured Party.** The assignment is not effective until the assignee (secured party) has given value. Value includes any consideration sufficient to support a simple contract, or a transfer in satisfaction of a pre-existing debt.

2) **Statute of Frauds for Other Assignments.** Other assignments that must be in writing include:

a) assignment of an interest in personal property or fixtures, for the purpose of security, as required by UCC Article 9;

b) any assignment of a right to personal property worth $5,000;

c) assignment of an interest in real estate;

d) assignment of a contract for the sale of goods with a price of $500 or more;

e) any wage assignment, if the jurisdiction permits such assignments to be made.

3) **Gratuitous Assignment**. Gratuitous assignments, made as a gift, are generally revocable. Gifts of tangible personal property are effective when there is donative intent combined with delivery of the property. In situations involving an assignment of an intangible right to payment of money, a chose-in-action, there is no tangible item that can be delivered.

a) **Delivery in Connection with Gratuitous Assignment.** Where there is some tangible item or writing, the possession of which generally represents ownership of the right, delivery of that writing, combined with donative intent, will effectuate the assignment and make it irrevocable. However, delivery of a check, by itself, is generally not regarded as an assignment of funds in the account.

Example: Uncle wishes to assign his bank account to his favorite Nephew. With the intent to make a gift, Uncle delivers possession of the passbook, required to be presented to make withdrawals, to the Nephew.

b) **Reliance on Assignment.** Reasonable reliance by the assignee on the assignment will make a gratuitous assignment irrevocable, at least to the extent of the assignee's reliance.

c) **Performance of the Obligation.** Performance of the obligation, such as by payment of the money involved, to the assignee, will also finalize a gratuitous assignment.

Example: Grandma tells Sally that the $1,000 her Uncle owes to Grandma is to be Sally's. Subsequently Uncle pays the $1,000 to Sally. Payment of the $1,000 makes the assignment irrevocable. Even before payment, the assignment would be irrevocable if Sally reasonably relied on the assignment, such as by making a contract to purchase a car for $1,000.

b. **Assignability of Rights.** Rights to receive performance or payment under a contract are generally freely assignable. Some rights, however, are not assignable where the assignment contravenes public policy or will materially change the obligations or risks to the obligor.

1) Wage Assignments Not Enforceable. In most jurisdictions wages may not be assigned. Because other rights to payment are assignable, the distinction between an employee, with a right to receive wages, and an independent contractor with a right to receive payment under his contract, is important.

2) **Assignments Materially Changing Obligation or Risk of Obligor.** Assignments which materially change the obligation or risk of the obligor are unenforceable. In contracts for the sale of goods UCC 2-210 makes rights

unassignable where the assignment would: 1) materially change the obligor's duty; 2) materially increase the burden or risk imposed on the obligor; or 3) materially impair the obligor's likelihood of receiving the return performance due under the contract.

a) **Insurance Contracts Not Assignable**. Assignment of an insurance contract, such as assignment of an auto collision policy by the owner of a car to his buyer, substantially changes the risk to the insurer and is not assignable.

b) **Contracts Involving Personal Services.** The right to receive performance of highly personal services may not be assigned, such as contracts for the services of a lawyer, accountant, doctor, musician or artist where the assignee may be more discerning or demanding than the assignor or the assignment would substantially alter the responsibilities of the obligor.

Example: Rex enters into contract with Photographer to take photos at his wedding. When he cancels his wedding he transfers his rights under the contract to Phil. Because of the artistic nature of the services involved, Rex's rights cannot be assigned.

c) **Contracts To Receive a Loan**. Rights of a borrower to receive a loan are generally not assignable where the financial condition of the borrower is a material aspect of the transaction.

d) **Requirements and Output Contracts**. Contracts for the sale of goods which measured the quantity by the buyer's requirements or the seller's output have traditionally been regarded as unassignable because of the impact an assignment of rights might have on the seller under a requirements contract or the buyer under an output contract. However, UCC 2-306, which removes a great deal of the subjectivity involved in such contracts, may make them more freely assignable than under prior law.

c. **Assignment of Future Rights.** Future rights were traditionally unassignable. However, Article 9 of the UCC permits free assignability of the right to payments under contracts not yet made as in a security interest in existing and after-acquired accounts receivable and chattel paper.

3. **Effect of Anti-Assignment Clauses.** Contracts sometimes include an express provision purporting to restrict assignment of the parties' rights. Anti-assignment clauses are generally ineffective to prohibit an assignment, though an assignment in violation of such a clause may be a breach that gives the other party the right to recover any damages from the assignor. Thus, an anti-assignment clause affects the assignor's right to make the assignment but does not deprive him of the power to make an effective assignment.

a. UCC 9-318(4) makes provisions prohibiting assignment of a contract for the **sale of goods or services** ineffective. It also makes ineffective any agreement which would prevent transfer of any other intangible right to payment as collateral for a loan. Any provision requiring the obligor's consent is similarly unenforceable.

b. UCC 2-210 treats general language prohibiting "assignments" as applicable only to a delegation of duties, and not as prohibiting a simple assignment of the right to payment.

Example: Agreement between Contractor and Homeowner for construction of a garage "prohibits assignment of the contract." This clause will be construed only to prevent Contractor from delegating his duties to perform and not to restrict his ability to assign his right to payment.

4. **Interpretation of Assignments and Delegations.** General language in an agreement indicating an assignment of "the contract" or of "the entire contract" or "all my rights under the contract" will be regarded as **both an assignment of rights and a delegation of duties,** unless the circumstances indicate otherwise.

a. **Assignment for Security**. An assignment to a financing agency or lender as security for a loan, or for financial purposes will be construed as involving only an assignment of the right to receive payment.

b. **Assignment of Rights Under Land Sale Contract.** A general assignment of rights under a land sale contract will not normally be interpreted as including both an assignment and a delegation.

c. **Partial Assignments.** An assignment of some, but not all of the rights due under a contract may be made even though they may present some inconvenience to the obligor who, if the partial assignment is effective, will find it necessary to split its payments or performance of other obligations. Still, so long as this inconvenience does not amount to a material change of its obligations, the partial assignment is effective.

5. **Assignments – Application of UCC Article 9 To Assignments of Accounts and Chattel Paper.** Article 9 of the UCC governs any assignment of an account or chattel paper, whether to secure an obligation or as an outright sale of the right to payment. Revised Article 9 also applies to assignments of payment intangibles and promissory notes.

a. **Accounts and Chattel Paper Defined.** Accounts and chattel paper are defined by UCC Article 9. Accounts and chattel paper should be distinguished from other types of payment rights, such as negotiable instruments governed by UCC Article 3, and "general intangibles" which are other rights to payment not involving an account, an instrument, or chattel paper, such as the right to receive book or music royalties, or an income tax refund.

1) **An account** is a right to payment for goods or services, regardless of whether the goods have already been delivered or the services have been performed.

2) **Chattel paper** consists of writings which include both: 1) a written right to receive payment, and 2) a security interest in or lease of specific goods.

Example: Retailer sells refrigerators, stoves, and dishwashers on credit to customers in three ways: 1) customers make a general promise to pay within 30 days of receipt of the goods; 2) customers sign a retail installment sales agreement giving Retailer a right to repossess the goods purchased if the customer does not make timely installment payments; and 3) customers charge the purchases on their Bank Credit Card. Retailer assigns his right to receive payments from the customers and from the Bank (under the credit card agreement) to Merchant's Finance Co., for cash. Transactions (1) and (2) involve accounts and chattel paper, respectively. Transaction (3) involves an assignment of a general intangible because it is a right to receive payment from the bank for money loaned. It should be noted that under **Revised UCC Article 9** credit card receivables of this type will be included in the definition of an "Account."

b. **UCC Terminology in Connection with Assignments.** UCC Article 9 uses its own terminology in connection with assignments of accounts and chattel paper and with assignments of other rights to payment for purposes of security.

1) **Debtor.** The "debtor" is the person to whom the right to payment is originally owed, referred to as the "assignor" under the common law. The assignor or seller of an account or chattel paper is known as the "debtor" even if the assignment was an outright sale with no "debt" or other obligation owed by the assignor.

2) **Secured Party.** The "secured party" is the assignee, the person to whom the right to receive payment is assigned. The assignee of accounts or chattel paper is known as the "secured party" even when the accounts or chattel paper are the subject of an outright sale involving no right of recourse against the assignor if the accounts or chattel paper are not fully collected.

3) **Account Debtor.** The "account debtor" is the obligor on the underlying contract, who owes the duty of payment under the account or chattel paper involved in the assignment.

Example: Auto Dealer sells cars to Customers on credit, retaining a security interest in the cars sold and obtaining a promissory note from the customers providing for installment payments. Auto Dealer sells the notes and security interests to Dealer Finance Corp. for cash with Dealer Finance Corp. taking over the collection of payments from Customers. This transaction involves a sale of chattel paper governed by UCC Article 9. The Auto Dealer is a "debtor"; Dealer Finance Corp. is the "secured party"; the Customers are "account debtors."

c. **Exclusion of Some Assignments of Accounts, Payment Intangibles, Promissory Notes, and Chattel Paper from Scope of Article 9.** Four types of assignments of accounts and chattel paper are excluded from the scope of UCC Article 9 and are therefore governed by the common law:

1) **Sale of a Business.** When accounts or chattel paper are assigned as part of the sale of the assignee's business which gave rise to the creation of the accounts or chattel paper, the assignment is not governed by Article 9.

2) **For Collection Only.** When the assignment is to a collection agency or otherwise for the purpose of collection only, UCC Article 9 does not apply.

3) **Assignment Accompanied by Delegation of Duties.** When a right to receive payment, represented by an account, is assigned together with a delegation of the duty to render the performance which earns the right to payment, UCC Article 9 does not apply.

4) **Assignment of a Single Account in Satisfaction of a Pre-existing Debt.** An assignment of an individual account to an assignee which is made in either whole or partial satisfaction of a pre-existing indebtedness is not subject to Article 9.

6. **Conflicting Priority of Multiple Assignees.** If a debtor (assignor) assigns the same accounts and chattel paper to more than one secured party (assignee), there will be a priority dispute between the two secured parties.

a. **Priority To the First To File or Perfect.** Priority is generally given, under UCC 9-312, to the first assignee to "file or perfect" its interest according to the rules of UCC Article 9. Perfection is most commonly accomplished by filing a **financing statement** in the office designated by Article 9. Perfection as to chattel paper can also be accomplished by taking **possession of the chattel paper.**

b. **Priority Over Chattel paper.** A secured party (assignee) can obtain priority over chattel paper, under UCC 9-308, even though the secured party was not the first to file or perfect if the secured party meets all of the following requirements:

1) **obtains possession of the chattel paper;**

2) for **new value;**

3) **in the ordinary course of his business**; and

4) The secured party acts **without knowledge** of the previously perfected security interest **or even with knowledge** if the previously perfected security interest is in the chattel paper **merely as proceeds** from the sale of inventory by the assignee.

7. **Obligor's Defenses against an Assignee**. When rights to payment are assigned, the obligor (or "account debtor") may wish to assert defenses or claims it has against the assignor in an action brought by the assignee to recover payment from the obligor. The traditional rule is that the "assignee stands in the shoes of the assignor," permitting the obligor to assert whatever defenses it had against the assignor against the assignee. UCC 9-318 changes this rule but only to a limited extent.

   a. **Defense of Payment**. Where the obligor (or "account debtor") has made payment to the assignor (or "debtor") the obligor will be able to assert this defense against the assignee (or "secured party") for payments made **before notification** to the obligor of the assignment has been **received**. When the obligor receives notification that the right to receive payment from him has been assigned he is entitled to insist on reasonable proof of the assignment and, unless proof is provided, may continue to make payments to the assignor.

      Example: Buyer purchased a lawn tractor mower from Hardware Store, promising in writing to make 12 regular monthly installment payments and giving Hardware Store a security interest in the tractor mower. After Buyer made 3 payments, Hardware Store assigned the right to Buyer's payments to Finance Co., but Buyer was not notified of the assignment. Buyer made 5 more payments to Hardware Store and was then notified of the assignment. Despite notice, Buyer made the remaining 4 payments directly to the Hardware Store. In an action brought by Finance Co, Buyer will be liable for the last 4 payments, even though she has already made payment to the Hardware Store, because these payments were made after Buyer received notice of the assignment. Buyer may recover payments made to Hardware Store on theory of restitution, to prevent unjust enrichment.

   b. **Defenses and Claims Based On the Transaction That Created the Account.** Absent an enforceable agreement not to assert defenses against an assignee, an obligor may assert any defenses and "claims in recoupment" that arose from the transaction that gave rise to the account. This will include any defenses based on fraud, breach of warranty, usury, or otherwise, so long as it is based on the same transaction that created the right to receive payment which was assigned.

      Example: Customer purchased auto from Dealer, on credit. Dealer assigned right to receive Customer's payment to Bank. The automobile was defective, in breach of Dealer's warranty of merchantability. Customer can assert the breach of warranty as a defense in an action brought by Bank to collect the amounts due under the agreement to purchase the auto.

   c. **Claims Based On collateral Transactions Between Obligor and Assignor.** With respect to claims arising from other transactions between the obligor and the assignor, the obligor may only assert defenses against an assignee based on claims or defenses that **accrued before the obligor received notification of the assignment.**

Example: Consumer purchased a Refrigerator from Appliance Store, on credit. Appliance Store assigned right to receive Refrigerator payments to Finance Co. Subsequently, Consumer purchased microwave oven from Appliance Store, paying cash. Consumer received notice of assignment of right to receive payment of Refrigerator Payments. Two weeks after receipt of notice of the assignment, the microwave blew up in violation of terms of Appliance Store's warranty. Because the cause of action on the collateral transaction, involving the microwave, accrued after Consumer received notice of the assignment, Consumer will not be able to assert its breach of warranty claim against the Finance Co. in Finance Co.'s action to recover payments due on the refrigerator. If the microwave had blown up before Consumer received notice of the assignment, Consumer would have been able to rely on breach of warranty claim to resist payment of amounts remaining due for the refrigerator.

d. **Agreements Not To Assert Defenses and Holder in Due Course Rules.** Agreements in a contract not to assert defenses against an assignee are enforceable by an assignee who took the assignment in good faith, for value, and without notice of the defense.

1) **FTC Rule.** A Federal Trade Commission Rule prohibits these "waiver of defense" clauses in connection with any sale or lease of goods to consumers.

2) **Close Connectedness Doctrine.** Moreover, any assignee who is **closely connected** to the assignor, such as by co-ownership or other close business relationship, may be treated as having **notice** of the obligor's defenses because of the close relationship, making the agreement not to assert defenses provision unenforceable by the closely connected assignee. This is the same FTC Rule and close-connectedness doctrine that prevents many transferees from acquiring **holder in due course status** under UCC Article 3.

Example: Consumer purchases home theatre system on credit from Home Theatre Dealer, promising to make installment payments. Agreement contains language by which Consumer "waives" the right to assert any defenses it has in any action brought by an assignee of the contract. Home Theatre Dealer assigns the contract to HTD Finance Co., which was organized to purchase such contracts made by Home Theatre Dealer and which is owned by the same parent corporation which owns Home Theatre Dealer and is managed by the same personnel as Home Theatre Dealer. The waiver of defense clause is ineffective. Inclusion of the waiver of defense clause violates the FTC's Holder in Due Course Rule and the close connection between the assignee, HTD Finance Co. and Home Theatre Dealer, puts HTD on notice of Consumer's breach of warranty defense.

e. **Modifications of Contract between Obligor and Assignor**. Circumstances may arise that make it necessary or useful for the parties to the original contract, the obligor and assignor, to modify the terms of their agreement. The common law permitted modifications, even those consisting of partial early payment partially discharging the obligor's duties, where they were necessary to enable the assignor to perform its obligations under the contract. UCC 9-318 permits any modification between the original parties (the obligor-account debtor and the assignor-debtor) if the modification is made **in good faith and in accordance with reasonable commercial standards** effective against the assignee.

Example: Contractor agrees to construct office building on Owner's property, with payment due from Owner upon completion of the work. Contractor then assigns right to receive payment from Owner, to Bank, in exchange for cash. Owner is notified of the assignment to the Bank. Subsequently, Contractor applies to Owner for advance payment to permit Contractor to complete the work and Owner agrees, making payment. Because the modification was in good faith and in accordance with reasonable commercial standards, and necessary to permit Contractor to complete the contract, the modification is enforceable against the assignee.

f. **Warranties of the Assignor**. The assignee is able to recover damages from the assignor, based on a theory of breach of warranty, where the assignee is unable to collect sums assigned by the assignor because of a defense caused by the assignor's conduct. Assignments carry with them the implied warranty that the rights assigned actually exist and are not subject to claims or defenses that will be effective against the assignee. An assignor provides a further implied promise that it will not engage in conduct that would adversely affect the ability of the assignee to collect. These warranties can, of course, be disclaimed by effective language.

1) **Recourse and Non-recourse Assignments**. The assignor does not normally make any warranty that the obligor will make payment or that the obligor will remain solvent. In a normal **"non-recourse" assignment**, the assignee has no right to recover from the assignor simply because the obligor fails to or is unable to pay. In a **recourse assignment**, however, the assignor makes an express promise to reimburse the assignee for any amounts unrecoverable from the obligor.

2) **Loans Secured By Rights To Payment.** When accounts, chattel paper, or other payment rights are not sold outright, but used as collateral for a loan from the assignee to the assignor, the assignee as a secured lender will have a right to recover a **deficiency** from the assignor, as debtor for any portion of the loan that is not paid through collections from the account debtor.

8. **Delegation of Duties.** A delegation of duties occurs when a party to a contract transfers his obligations to perform to another person who agrees to perform those duties.

a. **General Language of Assignment Refers To Rights and Duties.** General language assigning a contract will be interpreted, absent circumstances indicating a contrary intent, to include an **assignment of rights combined with a delegation of duties.**

b. **Person Making Delegation Remains Liable Absent Novation.** The person making the delegation, (sometimes called the delegator), remains liable for performance under the contract unless the person to whom the duty is owed agrees to a novation, releasing the original party to the contract from her responsibilities.

c. **Delegation Creates Third-Party Beneficiary Rights in Obligee.** A delegation in which a third party assumes the duties of an original party to the contract is a **third-party beneficiary contract**. The party to whom the original duties are owed stands as a third party beneficiary of the promise to assume the duties under the contract. Thus, the original party who made the delegation and the delegatee are both liable to the obligee.

d. **Non-Delegable Duties.** Duties are not delegable to third parties if the obligee has a **substantial interest** in receiving performance from the original party to the contract.

1) **Personal Services.** Contracts to provide personal services are the type of contract most likely to be non-delegable, particularly where the person who will provide the services has unique skill or where the services involved are those involving taste, judgment, or particular skill of the individual who will provide the service, or where the contract involves a material element of trust in the person who originally contracted to perform the services. However, where the services are not peculiarly personal, and are subject to objective evaluation, an otherwise non-delegable duty may be delegable if the original party to the contract will remain in business and actively supervise the performance by the delegatee.

Example: Contract between a Movie Production Company and Actor to appear in the lead role in a production of Hamlet. The Actor's duties are not delegable.

Example: Contract to provide architectural services in designing an office building, involving the personal skill and judgment of the architect, is not delegable, unless perhaps the original architect will supervise and control the performance of the delegatee.

Example: Contract to install and service soft drink vending machines in a restaurant was delegable to a third party even where the restaurant selected the original party because of his reputation for quality service.

2) **Prohibition against Delegation**. Language in a contract preventing the delegation of duties is generally enforceable.

9. **Novation**. A novation exists when there is a complete substitution of one party for another including a **release** of the original obligor. A novation requires the agreement of all of the parties to the agreement. It is distinguishable from a mere delegation in that after a novation the obligee has no remaining right to recover from the original obligor.

MBE Advice

In questions involving *third party beneficiaries*, you will often see an answer choice which is based upon the rules for *assignees* (and vice versa). Therefore, it is important to be able to distinguish between these two concepts. Remember that a *beneficiary* is created in the formation of the contract, whereas an *assignee* only gains his or her rights later, when a party transfers contractual rights to the assignee.

Printed in Dunstable, United Kingdom

91218885R00078